Endorsements

Understanding changes in the emerging culture of the Diaspora is the most crucial element in bringing faith, family and finances together for a harmonious living. Having been personally involved for many years with Asian Americans, I am thrilled to recommend this book to all Asian families and ministries, particularly to those who are working with Asians Indians.

Dr. Thomas Abraham
Vice President, Campus Crusade for Christ International

I am both a minister of the gospel and father of four grown children of the Coconut Generation. I am impressed with Sam George's striking insights and lessons that help us to relate and minister more effectively to them and their generation.

Rev. Dr. T. Valson Abraham
Founder/President, India Gospel Outreach

With a twinkle in his eye and a razor-sharp brain, Sam George asks young Indians in North America: Who are we? Where do we feel at home? How can we grow as Jesus' disciples? Sam provides a framework to find culturally relevant answers.

Miriam Adeney, Ph.D.
Associate Professor of Global and Urban Ministries,
Seattle Pacific University

Given the fact that the immigrant Indian American Christian youth in the postmodern dotcom culture are a social force to reckon with and a repository of intellect to draw from, the urgency to meaningfully cater to their needs is inescapable. Every sensible Christian leader of North America cannot but agree that there is no other alternative to Sam George's strategic advocacy.

Rev. Dr. Martin Alphonse
Assistant Professor of Intercultural Studies,
Multnomah Bible College and Seminary

To Elizabeth + Nich

from Mr Sam George -
(as your wedding gift)

Informative, insightful and timely, this is an essential resource for anyone seeking to learn more about the experience of and ministry among Americanized Asian Indians.

Peter Cha, Ph.D.
Associate Professor of Pastoral Theology,
Trinity Evangelical Divinity School

This book is one of a kind. The Asian Indian community will be indebted to the passionate plea of the author to look into the hearts and minds of the emerging generations in order to clearly understand them and lovingly minister to them.

Dr. David Chigurupati
President, National Association of Asian Indian Christians in USA

I have personally been enriched by the insights gained through chatting with Sam George about this important segment of the emerging religious landscape of North America which could be a powerful agent of renewal within the church at-large. I am happy that these insights are being made available to wider audience through this book.

Dr. Ajith Fernando
National Director, Youth for Christ, Sri Lanka

Jawaharlal Nehru's India was a "sleeping giant" but today's Indian Americans are a "throbbing giant" revving to go! Aptly qualified Sam George has brilliantly responded to a tremendous need, with careful observation, keen involvement and extensive research. The book is replete with trenchant insights and invaluable prescriptions for Indians and non-Indians alike.

Rabi Maharaj
Author, *The Death of a Guru*

The author offers an insightful analysis of the critical issues and challenges facing the children of immigrant Asian Indians. This book will help you in reaching them.

Naresh K. Malhotra, Ph.D.
Regents Professor of Marketing Management,
Georgia Institute of Technology

The writer is prolific with great insights and honestly addresses many critical issues. A must read for anyone who wants to understand, minister, and reach the South Asian youth.

Dr. Samuel Naaman
Founder-Director, South Asian Friendship Center

Anything from Sam George, read it. He is in the cutting edge of the modern missions which relates both to the East and the West. His understanding and ministry to the global Diaspora Indians is very informative. The Coconut Generation, the Desis in Videsh [Natives in Foreign] is a phenomenon which needs to be understood and dealt with. This book an excellent guide to that end.

Dr. K. Rajendran
General Secretary, India Missions Association

Sam George's analysis of the challenges of ministry to Asian Indians in America moves youth ministry to a new level as he engages the cultural challenge similar to but distinct from other immigrant groups and grounds his work in the theological framework of practical theology.

Mark H. Senter III, Ph.D.
Professor of Educational Ministries, Trinity Evangelical Divinity School

Finally.... a great resource which helps us better understand a new emerging group in a multicultural America. The book articulates with accuracy and credibility useable information which can be used for God, good and the advancement of the Great Commission. Great reading – which will inspire you to a new level of strategic purpose and intentionality.

Dr. Douglas Shaw
President/CEO, International Students Inc.

Sam George has spoken to his own younger generation (and beyond) with incisive wisdom and the grace of a reflective practitioner—one who acts and thinks, does and ponders, both globalized and grounded in his mother culture. Kudos to a creative title and graphic design.....for in this case artistic cover reflects substantive content.

Bill Taylor, Ph.D.
Executive Director, World Evangelical Alliance - Mission Commission

understanding the
COCONUT
GENERATION

understanding the
COCONUT
GENERATION
MINISTRY TO THE AMERICANIZED ASIAN INDIANS

SAM GEORGE

Mall Publishing, Co.
THE PRINTED WORD THE PLANTED SEED

NILES, ILLINOIS

Understanding the Coconut Generation:
Ministry to the Americanized Asian Indians
© 2006 by Sam George

Printed in the United States of America

Published by:
Mall Publishing Company
5731 West Howard Street
Niles, Illinois 60714
877.203.2453

Cover Design by Shajan Karottu
Book Design by Marlon B. Villadiego

Unless otherwise indicated, all scripture quotations are from the
Holy Bible: New International Version. Copyright © 1973, 1978, 1984
by International Bible Society. Used by permission.

Scripture marked Message is taken from The Message by Eugene
H. Peterson, copyright (c) 1993, 1994, 1995, 2000, 2002. Used by
permission of Navpress Publishing Group. All rights reserved.

ISBN 0-9777273-1-9

For licensing / copyright information, for additional copies
or for use in specialized settings contact:

Parivar International
P.O Box 5301
Vernon Hills, Illinois 60061
Phone: 847-362-1804
Email: info@coconutgeneration.com
Web: www.coconutgeneration.com

Table of Contents

Foreword

Massive immigration into America is a phenomenon of our times. It is no surprise that the most rapidly growing segment of the child population of American society is the first and second generation immigrant children. Immigration significantly transforms immigrant parents and their children while it also makes drastic changes in the host communities.

The escalating pace of immigration of Asian Indians and their growing influence in almost every major sphere of American life can no longer be ignored. The author invites us on a journey to boldly explore the critical issues and challenges facing the children of immigrant Asian Indians. Drawing from his personal observations, grassroots conversations, ministry reflections and scholarly research Sam George has provided us with a well-rounded, highly informative and practical volume. *Understanding the Coconut Generation* is a book long overdue.

As a serious student of culture, the Church and the Christian faith, the author with his caring heart and discerning mind carefully diagnoses the social and spiritual struggles facing the Coconut Generation. His conclusions echo what I have seen and heard in the Asian Indian community during my over three-decade itinerant ministry based on this continent. What is helpful are his prescriptions of contextual pointers for ministry and innovative emerging ministry models. He is also hopeful that by embracing necessary changes in our ministry approaches, the Christian faith of the Coconut Generation will not only survive but thrive. Many of the ministry insights presented here could be transferable and applied to the various contexts of the global South Asian Diaspora.

For Sam George this journey to deeper understanding of the emerging generation in order to serve them more effectively is still in progress. Hence he persuasively invites us to ponder over the questions he has raised and to join in the continuing online dialogue through the website.

I recommend this book with optimism and enthusiasm to all Asian Indian families and all (pastors, youth workers, community leaders, etc.) who meaningfully and redemptively relate with them.

Rev. Dr. T.V. Thomas

Co-Chair,
International Network of South Asian Diaspora Leaders (INSADL)

Acknowledgements

I am deeply indebted to many people who have played a crucial role in this project. My special thanks goes to Rev. Dr. T.V Thomas who has been instrumental in challenging the need for literature on second generation ministry and graciously agreed to write the Foreword. I am grateful to Bishop Euyakim Mar Coorilos for his enthusiastic support and kind endorsement of the book. Dr. Kenda Creasy Dean – an extraordinary teacher, theologian and mentor to me since seminary days whose passion for youth is a continual inspiration. Ram Gidoomal's many rich input from his Diasporic journey in Africa and Europe has been immensely valuable to me. I also thank all other endorsers for their kind and encouraging commendations.

I thank the Board of PARIVAR International, where I serve, in releasing me to pursue this writing. I greatly appreciate timely help from many people in this writing endeavor: Priya George and Shiji Mathew in proofreading and editing, Shoja Thomas for research and tabulations, Bobby Thomas for online survey, Stash John for the web design, Anil Thomas and Jerry Mathaikutty for promotions and Shajan Karottu for cover design. Most of all, I owe a great deal to the young people and youth leaders that I met all across North America. Your passion for God and extraordinary faith gives me a reason to believe that best is yet to come.

I praise God for my wife, Mary M. George - her loving support and encouragement keeps me going. I thank God for our children Daniel Ashish George and Joshua Anmol George, in a way this book is an attempt to understand them. I am grateful to Mary's dad, Mr. P.C. Mathew and my parents, Mr. & Mrs. K.S. George, for helping out with many household chores and taking care of our children, when I was engrossed in writing.

Above all else, I thank Jesus, who called me out of darkness, unto his marvelous light; life has never been the same since the day I had encountered him.

Preface

The United States of America has always been a nation of nations. So is India. In the USA it was on account of immigration and in India it is due to its inherent diversity of language, culture and religions. So if understanding Indian emigration to the United States is a complex matter, understanding the uniqueness of their descendents is even more complicated. Faith matters and insights for practical ministry to the emerging generations are harder to find. Because of their strong sense of religiosity, traditions, and family culture, the younger generation is caught between their ethnicity and assimilation tendencies. Quest of their unique identity and life purpose are beyond imagination of most adults in the community.

In spite of the pervasive presence of the American socializing agents such as public schools, churches, social organizations and popular media, the progenies of the immigrant generation stand outside of the mainstream society. They are neither here nor there, caught up in the complex web of influences and struggle without much help. They are looking everywhere for someone who understand their dilemma and help them navigate through the quagmire of bicultural adolescence.

This book is an attempt to understand the uniqueness of the second generation of the Asian Indian community and shape of the Christian ministry for and by them. Who are they really? Why make a big deal about them? Simply put, the Asian Indian second generation is different. They are different from their parents, their other American peers and their relatives back in India. They defy any standard categorization. Yet, they are so much like their parents! When we understand how they are the same and how they are different, we will be in a better place to serve them.

The book draws insights from many disciplines to develop a

comprehensive and integrated approach to this ministry to the emerging generations of Asian Indians in America. It begins with a brief historical analysis and refers to the latest demographical and sociological data from census and other agencies to determine the size and the background of the Coconut generation. It then moves to psychological and anthropological investigation to explore the identity and culture of the Coconut generation. In the following chapters it explores their sense of belonging, community, spirituality and some common struggles of this generation. Finally it develops a theological basis of doing ministry to this generation.

This book includes many stories of the emerging generation of Asian Indians in North America. Towards this book, a web-survey of youth leaders was conducted to glean lessons they have learned in serving their generation. It also comprises of the collective wisdom of youth pastors, parents, pastors and community leaders from all across the nation.

This is not the final word on this topic. Books have limitation of being a one-way communication tool. We would love to hear from you and interact with others interested in this area. We have developed a website www.coconutgeneration.com to facilitate further discussion on this topic, to network emerging leaders and to provide on-going updates on resources and training.

1

Cracking Open: Introduction to Coconuts

By blood and origin, I am an Albanian
By citizenship I am an Indian. I am a Catholic nun.
As to my calling, I belong to the whole world.
As to my heart, I belong entirely to Jesus.
– Mother Teresa.

The question of our ultimate heart allegiance is a complex one. It does not matter where we are born, what passports we hold, common perception of others or vocational commitments. Our deepest heart longing is to discover who we really are and who deserves our total allegiance in this world. This book is a humble attempt to reflect and understand who Americanized Asian Indians really are and how they can find eternal purposes in this increasingly complex world. It is a series of reflections interspersed with stories of Americanized Asian Indians in North America. Names have been changed to protect identities. I honestly tried to retell the stories of a generation and what I have learned from them about life, God, and Christian ministry. Right at the outset, I must admit that I have learned more from them than what I tried teaching them.

This book is the result of much persuasion, prayers and help of many youth leaders, pastors, parents, professors, and Christian workers of transplanted Indian churches and other Christian ministries. It is written to capture many facets of the second-generation experience and to glean insights for effective ministries to the future generation of the Indian-American community. I hope and pray this would enable further research and generate more publications about ministry in the Diasporic settings.

Who Are We Talking About?: More Than You Think

I refer to this generation as the "Coconut Generation" – 'brown on the outside, white on the inside.' This term is popularly used to describe the second generation of Asian Indians in Western-Caucasian cultures. I did not invent this term and its exact origin and extent of its usage are uncertain. Both in popular usage and in sociological literature, I have come across the term being used to describe the second generation Indians and other Americanized South Asians. This is only a figurative way to refer to this group and not intended at excluding people of other colors from the western countries nor use color in any racial or derogatory manner. I am painfully aware that some people feel strongly against the Coconut metaphor and like all metaphors this also could be twisted and misinterpreted. This symbolic usage is akin to Chinese Americans being called "Bananas" –'yellow from outside and white from inside'.

Another metaphor of this generation is *Chai* (Indian Tea) – a blend of brown extract from tea leaves and white milk. *Chai* is always taken with milk in India and once mixed together, the tea and milk cannot be separated. Unlike the Coconut metaphor, some think that for Americanized Asian Indians, the brownness and whiteness are so mixed together that there is no clear boundary between them. Like all metaphors, both "Coconut" and *"chai"* have its limitations and do not accurately represent this

2

generation. I simply like the vegetable theme and prefer to use that throughout this book in a representational manner.

Although the second generation is the major component, I hope to include couple of other groups in this conversation. As age or place of birth are inadequate criteria to describe a group comprehensively, I prefer to use culture as a primary defining issue for Americanized Asian Indians. Culturally not all second generation are Americanized, yet many who are born elsewhere show relatively

> Coconut (botanical name – Cocos Nucifera), is commonly seen in tropics worldwide. It is a slender, palm like tree with canopy of leaves on top. Copra (the dried "meat" of the seed), from which oil is extracted, is a significant cash crop throughout the tropics. Coir, the fiber from the fruit, is used in manufacturing. The fruits, or coconuts, yield several food products at different stages of development, and the leaves are used for thatch or are woven into baskets, mats and clothing. Even the trunks are used for construction.

higher cultural assimilation. So I include those who were born elsewhere and migrated to United States in their preteen years (popularly called 1.5 generation) and recent student immigrants who arrive quite americanized than immigrants of earlier era, in this conversation of ministry to the Americanized Asian Indians.

I do not claim to have figured out everything about this generation. This project has many shortcomings and I seek your apology for its limitations. Although I have interacted and learned from emerging Indian leaders in other parts of the world, I would limit most of the conversation in this book with the Indian American community. But there are many similarities and direct applications for emerging generations of Asian Indians all over the world. I pray that these thoughts will help you understand this generation better and serve them more effectively in their pursuit of discovering themselves and their purpose in this world.

Who Is The Author?: Just In Case You Wanna Know

I was born and raised in Port Blair, Andaman Islands – a group of islands in the Bay of Bengal, southeast of India. My parents hail from the state of Kerala in India and belong to the St. Thomas Christian traditions, the Mar Thoma Church in particular. Having grown up in a Kerala church transplanted in another culture, I had my own "second generation" experience. I simply knew that my generation was different from my parents. Without knowing much about these generational and cultural differences, my struggle has given me unique insights and empathy for the "second generation tribe" everywhere. During my professional studies and a career in software industry exposed me to the global Indian Diaspora in over fifteen countries and I learned first hand the tension between the immigrant generations and their descendents.

My early education was in Mechanical Engineering and graduate studies in Business Management. My professional career was in consulting and managing design software firms for nine years. Then, I studied at Fuller and Princeton Theological Seminaries. Currently, I provide leadership for a US based non-profit foundation involved in a number of charitable projects in Asia and Africa. I also serve as the Executive Director of PARIVAR International, a non-profit initiative committed to strengthen families in Asian Indian communities in North America.

Since the early '90s, I have been involved with the Indian community in United States in varying capacities. During this period I have lived in California, New Jersey and now in Illinois. I have served with a variety of youth ministries, churches, and para-church ministries. For a couple of years I served as the Youth Director with the Philadelphia Mar Thoma Church and am still involved with various youth and mission projects of the Mar Thoma Church. I have been involved with ministries in Brethren,

4

Indian Catholic, Indian Orthodox, Churches of South India (CSI), Evangelical, Pentecostal and many other independent Indian community churches all over the United States and have served young people in Gujarati, Hindi, Malayalam, Punjabi, Tamil and Telugu speaking congregations. I also had many opportunities to minister to young people in the United Kingdom and other Western countries. All these diverse involvements only proved my intuitions right about the cleavage and the spiritual struggle of migrant Indian communities, and I felt compelled to reflect and write this book for them. I hope to be balanced and objective in my analysis of the Indian American community.

Joining me in this journey and burden is my wife, Mary. We got married in 1996 and are parents of two boys. Mary is a research scientist and works for a Japanese American pharmaceutical company. We live in the northern suburbs of Chicago and are members of the Chicago Mar Thoma Church. We travel widely to minister in churches and ministries in the United States and beyond.

I am very hopeful of the Coconut Generation. I love young people and they have had a remarkable impact on my faith journey. Training and mentoring younger leaders is more than a passion for me. Their idealism, creativity, energy and commitment have left a lasting impression on me, and I am convinced that the best days for our community are ahead of us.

What It Is Not: Some Disclaimers

In the American context, sometimes the term Indian refers to the Native Americans or American-Indians. The confusion arose when Christopher Columbus sailed westward in the fifteenth century in search of India, subsequently discovered America, and

5

called the people there "Indians". This book is not about them, but about the "original" Indians from India. Ironically in the late twentieth century, Asian Indians discovered America as a place to study, work and raise their families. This book is the story of that adventure and the struggles of the emerging generation of Asian Indians in America.

Asian American is the popular term used to describe Asian immigrants in America and some literature on Asian American ministry includes Asian Indians perspectives, but very little has been written by them and for them. Asian Americans are an extremely diverse group of people to be put together for cultural analysis and ministry insights. Indian-American is another term I would use to refer to Asian Indians in America and it should not be mistaken for Native Americans.

It does not include the so-called first wave of immigrants from India in late nineteenth and early twentieth centuries. Most of the reflection is on the children of post-1965 second wave of immigrants from India. I have tried to record stories of Christian communities from various parts of India.

Though I have done expansive research, some readers may interpret some of my viewpoint as broad generalizations. They might not necessarily be true of your experience or observation, and I fully concur with your right to disagree with some of those sweeping statements. However, for the sake of understanding a generation, I have taken the risk of some generalizations.

This is not a sociological or psychological analysis of an immigrant community, although it does contain some of it. Neither is this a youth ministry or parenting 'how-to' guide, but there are many insights that could come in handy. This is not about church planting nor a theological treatise, but a sub-cultural analysis that could help our practical ministry to the emerging generation of the Indian American community.

What Is It Then: What to Expect

This is an interdisciplinary account of the Indian American experience, including brief historical review, demographic data, socio-psychological analysis, anthropological and theological reflections, and lessons for ministry. It is concerning identity formation, subculture, family issues, community, spiritual growth and church experiences of the Americanized Asian-Indians in the United States of America. It contains comparative analysis with other immigrant experiences and mainstream American youth ministries, for lessons in ministering to the emerging generations of Asian Indians.

> **A battle is raging for a generation of young people and winner owns the future. If we do not join the battle, we forfeit a generation and our future.**
> **Ron Hutchcraft**

It explores the identity formation process and complexities involved from various perspectives. It aims to locate what goes on inside the mind and heart of a second generation: Who am I - Indian or American? Which comes first? How will that influence my belief system and religious affiliation? Will the emerging generation preserve the Indian culture and religious traditions? How do the Asian Indians construct their American identity? How do Indian-Christians integrate conflicting identities of being Christian, Indian and American? What are some common struggles between the generations?

Although this is written from a Christian ministry perspective, the second-generation experiences are drawn from a much broader setting. Pastors, youth leaders and Sunday school teachers will profit most from this resource. However, this will also offer help to parents, educators, social workers, counselors and other who work with children and youths from all religious backgrounds.

Many of these transferable concepts are applicable to the emerging generations of Indians in other global contexts.

I hope this book will be a catalyst for further dialog and to develop deeper understanding regarding issues pertaining to the Coconut generation. I invite you to join the online community at the web site – www.coconutgeneration.com. The site aims to continue the conversations on emerging generation, culture, and ministries in order to create an electronic repository of issues pertinent to the Coconut generation. The site will provide regular updates and network leaders, thinkers and practitioners in this area.

What Is The Basis: Biblical Purposes

I was greatly encouraged to discover that Bible has much to say about emerging generation and is relevant to our contemporary issues. Three Scripture passages come to mind. This book can be best described in the words of prophet Malachi – "turn the hearts of fathers to their children and the hearts of children to their fathers" (Mal 4:6). And more importantly, turning the heart of both generations to the Living God of the Universe.

It is said of David that when he had "served God's purpose in his own generation, he fell asleep." (Acts 13:36) It is my prayer that the second generation of Asian Indians in Diasporic setting would serve God's greater purposes for their generation before they fall asleep. A generational thrust in ministry is very strategic and critical in all migratory communities.

And finally, I hope that the emerging generations of Asian Indians will be like men of Issachar, who "understood the times and knew what Israel should do." (1 Chronicles 12:32). May there be many from the Coconut generation who understands our ever changing times and know what they should do in order to leave behind a lasting spiritual legacy in our community and the world.

Allow me to introduce you to the future (or should I say the present). Come, let us plunge into it together...

To Ponder About:

1. What is your interest in the subject of this book (Americanized Asian Indian Ministries)? What do you hope to learn from this book?

2. According to you, who are Americanized Asian Indians? What characterizes them? How are they same or different from others around you?

3. What are pros and cons of using the metaphor "Coconut" for Americanized Asian Indians?

2

Roots - Routes:
Origin and Journeys of Coconuts

Mera juta hai Japani, mera pathloon hi angrezi
Sar pe lal topi Roosi, phir be dil he Hindustani.
(my shoes are Japanese, my trousers are English
Cap on my head may be Russian, but my heart is still Indian.)[1]

When Pico Iyer, a second generation Asian Indian travel
writer was asked, "Where do you come from? And where is
home?" his reply was a perplexing one, "I am 100% Indian by
blood and heritage. Most of my relatives live in India, my family
name places me very specifically in terms of caste and region and
religion, and everything about my face shouts out, unanswerably,
'India!' Yet I've never lived in India or worked there. I speak not
a word of any of the country's 1,652 dialects. And when I return
to what is, on paper at least, my ancestral home—Bombay—I
feel more a stranger there, than do many of my friends from San
Francisco or North London. Ask me to take a journey home, and
my first question is: do you mean Oxford, England (where I was
born), or California (where I keep my things and pay my taxes)?
Or do you mean Japan (my adopted home, where I spend seven
or eight months of every year)? The one place that does not come
to mind is India!"[2]

The complex nature of the life of the Coconut generation forces us to explore both our cultural *roots* and the migrationary *routes* we have taken – where we came from, how we got here, where we are now, and why all that matters. Our origin and the journeys we undertook paint an indelible mark on our current consciousness and will guide us to our future. No matter what we wear, what languages we speak or passports we hold, our deepest heart longing is beyond all these defining issues. Nevertheless, our roots and routes are critical in our quest for identity and meaning.

This chapter contains some statistics and demographical data and if it gets to be overwhelming please skip over to the next section. It is important to know who we are talking about and substantiate it with some real numbers. At any case, do not miss the essence of the chapter in the last four sections.

Wandering People: Sojourners

The human history is filled with stories of people wandering around the world. Our ancestors moved to new places looking for food, water, livelihood and security. Some moved seasonally with the grazing needs of livestock, while others were forced to migrate due to famine or other natural disasters. Nomadic lifestyle was nothing new to them. Explorers looked for new places over land and sea; wars and conquests, slavery, expulsion, exile, colonization, and forced resettlement have all caused dispersion of people everywhere. All migrations have changed people on account of giving and taking of cultures and beliefs.

The Asian countries had its share of wandering people; Indian and Chinese herbs and medicines were well sought after in the Middle East and the rest of Asia. Sea routes over the Arabian Seas and the Indian Ocean to Africa and East Asia can be traced back to the pre-Christian era. The contributions of ancient Indian civilization to the world of science, mathematics, philosophy and art are well known. From early historians, it is evident that people from the region, that we know today as India, also traveled far and wide. Indians also had visitors from all over the world come to its shores. Some came for trade while others overpowered the local kings and ruled India. The European colonial era brought Portuguese, French, and most significantly, the British to India in the nineteenth and early twentieth century.

Today, the United States of America is the largest and most favored destination for migrant masses globally. The US has the largest foreign born population in the world (in 1990 it was 19.6 million, 8% of the total population & in 2003, it has grown to 33.5 million; 11.7% of the population[3]). The vibrant economy, education, opportunities, and the free society make an attractive proposition for people everywhere to emigrate.

Asian-American is the fastest growing immigrant community in the United States. The number of Asian Pacific Islander Americans is ex-

> **The sun never sets on the Indian Diaspora.**

pected to triple between 1990 and 2020, bringing Asian Americans themselves to 8% of the total U.S. population. Some of the Asian countries sending migrants globally include the Philippines, Taiwan, Japan, South Korea, Malaysia, Vietnam, Pakistan, Sri Lanka, Bangladesh, India and China. Today, Chinese and Indian are the largest migrant communities in the world, quite understandable considering the billions of people there are in these countries.

The Indian Diaspora stretches across all the oceans and the continents. The colonial legacy of language, forced migration, modernization, and technology industries have enabled Indians to get scattered all over the world. The influence of Indian culture is still strongly felt in South East Asia after many centuries. One could find Asian-Indians in almost every part of the habitable world. They are so widespread that the sun never sets on the Indian Diaspora, akin to the British Empire in the past!

Like the Jews and Chinese, the global Indians are building a networked civilization, an archipelago of nodes linked together by "Indian-ness" and aided by technology. The global Indian Diaspora is being knit together and held in place by the shared cultural space. The literature of the Diaspora tops best-seller lists and fusion food is served at the trendiest restaurants in London and New York. The popular glue of Bollywood (and its siblings Tollywood, Mollywood etc.) has played a crucial role in creating a universal consciousness of the subcontinent.

Non-Resident Indians: People of Indian Origin (NRI/PIO)

A non-resident Indian (NRI) is an Indian citizen who has migrated to another country. Other terms with the same meaning are overseas Indian and expatriate Indian. For tax and other official purposes, the Government of India considers any Indian national away from India for more than 180 days in a year as a NRI. In common usage, this often includes Indian-born individuals who have taken the citizenship of other countries. A Person of Indian Origin (PIO) is literally, a person of Indian origin who is not a citizen of India. The Indian government issues a PIO Card for anyone of Indian origin upto four generations.

The population of the Indian Diaspora is estimated to be about twenty million[4]. Some others project it as high as 25 million. See Appendix A1 for population of global Indian Diaspora. In ten countries there are more than half a million persons of Indian descent and they represent a significant proportion of the population of those countries. Their industry, enterprise, economic strength, educational standards, and professional skills are widely acknowledged. They live in different countries, speak different languages and are engaged in different vocations. What marks their uniqueness is their Indian origin, the consciousness of their cultural heritage and their deep attachment to family back in India. They had been so successful economically that just a few years ago the twenty million people earned more than the GDP of India (i.e. earning of a billion people back home)!

During the nineteenth century and until the end of the colonial rule, much of the migration that happened was of a forced nature. Indians were exported as laborers to other colonies under the indenture system. The major destinations were Mauritius, British Guyana, Trinidad, Jamaica, Fiji, South Africa and Malaysia. The British *Raj* employed Indian foot soldiers in the First and the Second World War.

Soon after India's independence in 1947, Indians went by choice for jobs and business to Eastern African nations like Kenya, Tanzania, Uganda and other Commonwealth nations like Australia, United Kingdom and Hong Kong. The oil economy of the Gulf countries drew many engineers and technicians from India in the nineteen sixties. The need for skilled labor forced America and western European nations to open its doors to Indian professionals like doctors, engineers, nurses and scientists. From the eighties young Indians went overseas for higher education, mostly to the United States, United Kingdom and Australia. With the global technology revolutions in the nineties, America absorbed a large number of Indian software professionals. The successes of the Indian Diaspora can be attributed to its traditional ethos, its cultural values and heritage, its educational aptitude and qualifications, and its capacity to harmonize and adapt. In several countries, NRIs have surpassed the per capita income of the indigenous population and hold very influential positions in the society.

15

The presence and influence of Indians in Trinidad for over 150 years is evident by the proclamation of "Indian Arrival Day" as a permanent national holiday by the government of Trinidad. In recognizing the dispersed people of Indian origin, the government of India has declared January 19th of every year as the Overseas Indians Day (*Parvasi Barathiya Divas*). On this day in 1914, Mahatma Gandhi returned to India from South Africa and gave leadership to the freedom struggle against the British colonial rule.[5]

Asian Americans: Who?

Indians generally get clubbed together as Asian Americans. The term 'Asian American' is a continental reference to the place of origin, just like Euro-Americans and Afro-Americans. This notion assumed that all Asians are a homogenous people group and creates a hyphenated identity like all other immigrants. Strictly speaking the Asian American reference should include not only dominant ethnic groups like Chinese, Japanese, and Koreans, but also sub-continental regions like South Asia, South East Asian, Central Asian nations and Pacific Islands. In fact, Asia comprises of over 50 countries and almost 4 billion people with various ethnic, cultural, linguistic and religious backgrounds. Such lumped categorization only helps to garner greater political clout, government funding and professional networking. It is of very little help for understanding a particular sub-group or drawing out ministry insights. As various Asian ethnic populations increased in America, the ethnic- or nation-specific hyphenated identity emerged as a helpful corrective.

In 2000, there were over 10 million people from Asia living in the United States. Over one quarter of all foreign-born Americans were from Asia. Chinese are the largest Asian entity – 2.43 million (including people from Taiwan) and Filipino being the next in size – 1.85 million. Asian Indians makes the third largest group with 1.68 million[6]. As compared to 1990, Indians have become the fastest growing Asian community in America. Besides these dominant nations, Asian migration is also comprised of people like Vietnamese, Koreans, Cambodians, Malays, Indonesians, Thais, Laosians, Pakistanis, Sinhalese, Arabs, Bangladesis, Nepalis, Tibetans, and many other smaller nations.

The immigrants from some of the smaller sub-regions of Asia can be located throughout the United States and often overlooked in the discourse on Asian Americans. They do not appear on most radars as they lack critical mass. It could also be bias against minority groups on account of low numerical and economic strength and hence political representation. It might not be intentional, but that is how it seems for outsiders in a foreign land.

Chart 1: Asian American Population

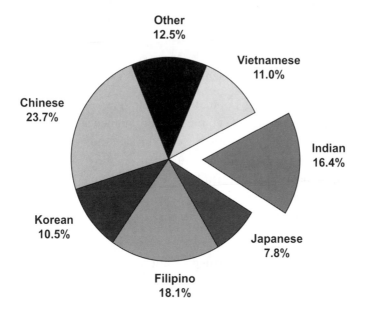

Other
12.5%

Vietnamese
11.0%

Chinese
23.7%

Indian
16.4%

Korean
10.5%

Japanese
7.8%

Filipino
18.1%

Contrary to the American scene, the term British Asian is commonly used to describe South Asians in the United Kingdom, who are the largest Asian immigrant community there. This term eclipses Chinese, Koreans, Filipinos and Japanese. Likewise the focus of Asian studies in the United States is pre-occupied primarily on Chinese, Japanese and Koreans, while overlooking South Asians and others.

The challenge of nomenclature of immigrant population is an on-going struggle and is evident in the conclusion that Dr. Vinay Lal, the professor of History at the University of California Los Angeles made, "The earlier nomenclature of "Hindoos" for all Indians had long been abandoned, but their designation as "Indians" was scarcely more acceptable, since what are now known as "Native Americans" were also known as "Indians". The term "Asian American" was not much in vogue, and in any case referred primarily to those from the Far East (and later South East Asia); and unlike in Britain, where Indians appeared to tolerate being lumped together with Africans and Caribbean people as "black", even deriving new political coalitions and formations in the common interest of combating oppression, in the United States the designation "black" was seen as condemning one to membership in a permanent underclass."[7]

With the swelling population of immigrants from India and sensing the value of ethnic-specific nomenclature, the U.S. Census created a new category called Asian Indian in 1980, (they were known as East Indians until then). In the early 1990s Asian Indians moved from fourth largest of the Asian American group to third largest.[8] They also stand out among Asian Americans for their balanced gender ratio because of the family reunification provisions of immigration.

The Asian American categorization may serve political and sociological analysis, but is too broad for mapping a particular culture or for gleaning ministry lessons. Of course, there is much to learn from other Asian American ministries and that is why I have designated chapter 8 to it. Even South Asia is a broad classification to study the faith of the emerging generation, due to various religious and cultural differences. Although this writing mostly applies to Indians, some of the characteristics of the emerging generation could be extended to Asian Americans at large.

Table 1: Asian population in the United States (1990 – 2000)[9]

	1990	% of Asian	2000	% of Asian	1990-2000	% change
Indian	815, 447	11.8	1,678,755	16.4	863,318	105.9
Chinese	1,645,472	23.8	2,432,585	23.7	787,113	47.8
Filipino	1,406,770	20.4	1,850,314	18.1	443,544	31.5
Japanese	847,562	12.3	796,700	7.8	(50,862)	-6.0
Korean	798,849	11.6	1,076,872	10.5	278,023	34.8
Vietnamese	614,547	8.9	1,122,528	11.0	507,981	82.7
Other Asian	779,991	11.3	1,285,234	12.5	505,243	64.8
Total Asian	6,908,638		10,242,998		3,334,360	48.3%

Although there exists many similarities between South Asians and East Asians (like strong emphasis on education, work ethics, religiosity and family oriented culture), still the differences are too glaring to consider them as a homogenous group. They are different in matters of race, religion, ethnicity and socio-economic class. The East Asian culture is largely shaped by the philosophy of Confucius, whereas South Asian culture is mostly shaped by

Hinduism. The East Asians are mostly Mangloid race, while most South Asians are Aryan and Dravidian race. Ethnicity varies widely across the Asian region and most major religions of the world find their origin in Asia. Judaism and Christianity in Israel, Islam in Arabia, Confucianism in China, Hinduism, Buddhism, Sikhism and Jainism in India, Shintoism in Japan. No wonder Asians are said to be religious in their outlook.

India sends the largest number of immigrants annually to the United States from the South Asian region. I have chosen to focus on people from India and not include people from other South Asian nations like Bangladesh, Bhutan, Maldives, Nepal, Pakistan and Sri Lanka. However, many of the lessons from this book are transferrable to communities from South Asian nations in America.

Table 2: Major South Asian Migration to USA[10]

Year of Admission to United States	India	Pakistan	Bangladesh	Sri Lanka
1946-1964	6319	1310	-	-
1965	582	187	-	-
1970	10114	1528	-	242
1980	22607	4265	532	397
1990	30667	9729	4252	976
2000	42,046	14,535	7,215	1,123

Chalo Amrika[11]: **The First Wave**

The earliest Asian Indian presence in America is for anybody to guess. But by the late nineteenth century, there were many recruitment drives for laborers to work in the lumber towns of Washington, laying railroads in Oregon and working in the agricultural fields of California. By 1920, some sixty-four hundred Indians had entered the United States.[12] This is often referred to as the first wave of Indian immigration. Most of the early immigrants were single men, the men to women ratio were almost seventy-five to one and many ended up marrying Mexicans or other ethnic immigrants. They were prohibited from marrying white women. In 1914 women represented 0.24 percent of the 5000 Asian Indians in California. Many married men had left their wives and children behind in India in order to pursue their American dream.

The inscription on the Statue of Liberty offers this invitation, "Give me your tired, your poor, Your huddled masses, yearning to breathe free, The wretched refuse of your teeming shore, Send these, the homeless, tempest tossed, I lift my lamp beside the golden door." This might have been true for the first wave of Indian immigrants, but this idea was soon to be toppled by the new wave of immigrants; when ambitious, well-educated professionals from free democratic India huddled the shores of America, only limited by their dreams.

> **Some push us around, some curse us**
> **Where is your splendor**
> **and prestige today?**
> **The whole world calls us black thieves,**
> **The whole world calls us 'coolie'**
> **Why doesn't our flag fly anywhere?**
> **Why is there no respect for**
> **us in the whole world?**
>
> **A protest song from the Gadr Movement by the first wave of Indian immigrants in America.**

Pursuing the Dream: The Second Wave

The liberalization of the US Immigration Act in 1965 opened a new chapter in the history of immigration, particularly for Asians in the United States. When for centuries the majority of America's immigrants were Europeans, these fundamental shifts in policy began to tilt the aspirants from Asia, even to the extent that one out of two immigrants come from Asia. The Act abolished the national origins system replaced by a hemispheric quota system. The new system was most favorable to Asians, especially Chinese, Koreans, Indians, Filipinos and Vietnamese, making them the largest and fastest growing immigrants in America. The new laws provided the push to increased migration from the Indian sub-continent, particularly India recording a steep rise in its population from 10,000 in 1965 to 525,000 twenty years later and crossing the million- mark in 1997.

According to the 2000 US Census[13], about 1.7 million people reported race as Asian Indian and an additional 200,000 reported Indian American combination with another race. It is almost 16% of the Asian American population and 0.6% of the entire US population. The Indian American population roughly doubled since the census of 1990. 96.7% of Indian Americans live in urban areas and 64.4% of the population lives in ten metropolitan cities (see table 3). One-third of all foreign born Indian Americans arrived in the United States between 1995 and March 2000 (time of the census). 27.07% of all Indian Americans were born in United States and another 29.04% have become naturalized citizens. Both of which adds up to 56.11% of all Indian American are US citizens, totaling to 1.07 million. The median age of the Indian American population is 30.3 years and 24.8 % falls below the age of 18 and 71.4% between the ages of 18 and 64. Of the total Indian American population, 18.2% arrived in the US before 1980 and another 27.8% between 1980 and 1989 and the remaining 54% arrived between 1990 and 2000.

Unlike the early Indian immigrants who came mostly to California, Indians who came after 1965 were scattered all over America, but mostly in big cities like New York, Philadelphia, Jersey City, Chicago, Houston, Dallas, Los Angeles, Washington DC, etc and other smaller cities. The post-1965 Asian immigrants are generally more geographically dispersed, better educated and better off economically than pre-1965 Asian immigrants.[14] Today, one can find Indians in the remotest parts of Arizona, New Mexico and even Alaska.

The second wave of newcomers was strikingly different from the earlier immigrants. Unlike the railroad workers and farm laborers of the first wave of immigrants, the second wave immigrants were more educated, highly skilled and came with job related experience. The latter were urban professionals while the former were rural farmers. The second wave immigrants pursued careers in high technology and service industries. They came with their families or brought them soon afterwards while in the earlier wave it was mostly single men. When their predecessors were native Indian language speakers, the later immigrants were fluent in English and performed well in cross-cultural work settings. They also arrived as settlers rather than sojourners. Since the change of immigration rules, the Indian community has shown steady growth in their numbers and proportionately far higher than the first wave of immigration to America.

The majority of Asian Indians are managers, professionals, executives and small business owners. Professionals include doctors, nurses, paramedics, pharmacists, engineers, scientists, professors, bankers, software developers, management, etc. The elite socio-economic profile should not be mistaken to represent Indians back home. America got the cream of the crop of Indian brain. Taught and trained in leading medical institutions, Indian Institute of Technology and other engineering colleges, combined with high motivation to excel, they did exceedingly well in the adopted country.

Table 3: Ten Largest Metropolitan Areas
by Indian American Population[15]

Metropolitan area	Metro Area Population	IA Population	IA Pop % of Metro Area	% of National IA Population
New York	21,199,865	453, 896	2.14	23.89
San Francisco	7,039,362	158,396	2.25	8.34
Chicago	9,157,540	125,208	1.37	6.59
Los Angeles	16,373,645	121,745	0.74	6.41
Washington	7,608,070	98,179	1.29	5.17
Houston	4,669,571	57,158	1.22	3.01
Philadelphia	6,188,463	57,124	0.92	3.01
Dallas/Ft. Worth	5,221,801	53,975	1.03	2.84
Detroit	5,456,428	49,879	0.91	2.63
Boston	5,819,100	48,188	0.83	2.54

The bright, educated, and ambitious men and women were more likely to explore opportunities overseas. From the early 1970s through the mid 1980s, more than 15,000 engineers and more than 15,000 physicians came to America.[16] The "Brain Drain" came to define the 80s and 90s, when the smartest young people came to American universities for higher education or to work in the high-tech industries. Like many developing nations, India produced more professionals than it could employ. After the liberalization of Indian economy in the early '90s, a reverse brain drain phenomena began to happen, popularly called 'brain gain'. Many professionals with American education and professional experiences in cutting-edge industries returned to set up businesses and market Indian skills worldwide.

24

The educational achievement of Asian Indians is the highest of any ethnic group in America.[17] Almost 65% of the entire Indian American population has at least a Bachelor's degree and 21% Masters and almost 5% Doctorate. Over 15% is enrolled in college or graduate school, again highest of all categories. About 60% of Indian Americans are involved in management, professional and related occupations as compared to 34% of the total US population. The earning of Asian Indians is the highest in the US, exceeding even the Japanese who were the top earners for many decades[18]. The median household income $70,708, while the general population median is $41,994.

Indians in the USA are probably the most well-off among the global Indian Diaspora - their median income is more than 1.5 times that of the host country and boasts of 200,000 millionaires. They are well represented in all walks of life, but particularly so in academia, information technology, and medicine. Over 5000 Indian professors teach and research in American universities. The Indian students have overtaken Chinese students to become the largest ethnic student group in the universities. The American Association of the Physicians of Indian Origin boasts a membership of 35,000. In 2000, *Fortune* magazine estimated the wealth generated by Silicon Valley Indian entrepreneurs at around $250 billion.

Despite such remarkable socio-economic advancements, the Indian community has its share of problems. Racism is one. Perhaps the worst example being the New Jersey "dot busters" - groups of thugs who sought ethnic Indians and mugged them or attacked their property in the late 80s and early 90s. The "dot" was a reference to the *bindi* worn by Hindu women on their forehead. In Post-9/11 America, men in the Sikh community came under suspicion for their long beard and turban. The tendency of some Indian Americans to retain a strong cultural identity while socializing within their own community and reluctance to integrate into mainstream society might have contributed to the problem of racism.

Another important piece of data that is particularly relevant to the study of ethnic youth is that there are significant incidences where Indian American children live in poverty, contrary to the popular notion that Indians in America are all affluent. Nationwide 10.13% of Indian American children under the age of 17 years old and 23.04% of Indian Americans aged 18-24 live in poverty.

Diversity Among Indians: United by Differences

The term *Desi* came to self describe the Indians in America, which in Hindi means from "our own country." It is derived from *Desh*, meaning nation in Hindi; *desi* simply means belonging to a nation; an Indian version of 'country cousin'. Another term that has come to define the second generation of Indians in America is *ABCD*, acronym for American Born Confused *Desis*. This is akin to American Born Chinese, but used somewhat derogatorily of their identity confusion. More recently the acronym has been redefined as American Born Confident *Desis*.

The people of Indian origin in the United States are culturally diverse. Most Americans are oblivious of the distinctions and often generally categorized as 'Indian'. The differences are associated with respect to places that they hail from and various cultural and religious extractions. Another mistake often made about people of Indian origin is that they migrated directly from India. This is certainly not the case. Some had circuitous migratory journeys as they went to Gulf countries, European countries, Africa, Australia, Canada, South East Asia, etc. before migrating to the United States. Such two or more step migration further complicates their cultural identity profiles due to multiple assimilation patterns.

The language is an important differentiator among Indian immigrants. Around 1980, Indians in the New York area could be divided by language as Gujurati (34%), Hindi (20%) and Dravidian languages, four south Indian languages – Malayalam, Tamil, Telugu and Kannada (24%). During the same time, in Southern California, there were 20% of Indians spoke Punjabi and Gujarati, 18% spoke Urdu, 16% were Hindi speakers, 12% spoke four of the southern Indian languages and 11% spoke Bengali (includes people from Bangladesh also).[19] During the late 70s, there were many Malayalam speakers from South India working in healthcare industries, in the 80s many entrepreneurs in the hospitality industry were Gujaratis while the late 90s saw a relatively large portion of Telugu speaking immigrants in computer-related industries.

Indian immigrants in the US are also divided along the lines of caste, religion, region, political persuasion, socio-economic status etc. Most Indians can identify fellow immigrant's background like language, religion, caste, state that they hail from etc, from his or her name. Adherents of various religious persuasions can be located in most cities and are more diverse than any other ethnic community. Temples dedicated to various Hindu deities, churches of various Indian denominations, Mosques, and *Gurudwaras* have become a permanent feature of the urban landscape of America.

The knowledge and skill levels of Indian Americans are varied and can be located in every walk of life - Nobel laureates, policy makers, global governance, newsstand owners, scientists, travel agents, politicians, journalist, healthcare pros, academics, musicians, religious gurus, gas station attenders, economists, software programmers, cab drivers etc.

Another glaring misnomer is that all Indians in America are

highly educated and wealthy. Although it is true that the average income of Asian Indians is the highest among ethnic minorities in America as previously mentioned, Indians are represented in all socioeconomic levels. There are very wealthy and very poor, but the majority belongs to the middle class. The average income is higher than the national average due to dual income homes and jobs in high paying industries. But there are Indians who live in abject poverty without any education or job, deplorable living conditions and without health benefits. Ironically, their families and relatives back home think that because they are in America they are minting money. As a result, they are too ashamed to go back to visit relatives and choose to suffer silently here.

Some Indians are more enterprising than others. They have made aggressive inroads in industries like hospitality, travel, spice, real estate etc. The retail outlets of Indian sweets, clothing, groceries, sari and jewelry provide handsome returns. Many of the merchants are relatives of professionals who came to America earlier. In the nineties, technology entrepreneurs reaped rich dividends during the IT boom. One interesting area where Indian Americans dominate is in the hotel/motel business ranging from cheap inner city hotels, to franchises, to well-known hotel chains along the interstate highways. As early as 1987, the *Wall Street Journal* reported that 28 percent of all motels in the United States were owned by Asian Indians[20] and by 2003 owning over 18,000 hotels across America with a market value of $38 Billion.

What Brought Indians to America: More than A Dream

Economic opportunity is undoubtedly the primary reason behind all people movements around the world today. Other reasons could include religious persecution, natural disasters, or political asylum. Whether it be water sources or greener pastures, people go where they could potentially make better livelihood. Compared to the earning of the first wave immigrants in early 1900, Rev. Wherry concluded, "Men receiving from 5 to 8 cents a day in India, by emigrating to America and working in the fruit orchards and sawmills they could make from seventy five cents to two dollars a day."[21] Almost a century later, the same wage ratio is a powerful attraction to Indian emigration to the United States. An Indian software professional who makes two thousand dollars a year in Indian dreams of exploring employment opportunities in America for a forty thousand dollar annual salary.

Most Indians enter the United States under three categories: employment, student or sponsorship by relatives. Most post-1965 immigrants came alone to America and subsequently sponsored their spouses and children. One of the unique trends of the Indian migration to the United States in the sixties and seventies was that many women came first to work in the healthcare industries. Most of them were Indian Christians who were professionally trained in hospitals and institutions established by Christian missionaries. Although far from India, they felt secure to migrate to a 'Christian' nation and work in professional environments.

Another major reason to emigrate was the lack of opportunities in India. The employment opportunities were severely limited and large numbers of educated, unemployed professionals were forced to look 'outside.' Many who came to America were also forced to work in areas outside of what they were originally trained for. Some obtained minimal training and exposure on the side to enhance their prospects. Many were forced to venture into low risk, low capital small businesses and worked hard over a long period of time.

A strong emphasis on education prevails among all Indians. Pursuing education in the United States has been a continual attraction as career prospects improves considerably with American degrees. So it was not surprising that since 2001 the Indian student enrollment has exceeded all other foreign born student populations in American universities. Indians now account for 13.9 percent of international students on American campuses. However, India's rate of increase this year has slowed from last year's 12 percent growth.

Table 4: Foreign Students in the USA (2003-04)[22]

Country	Students	Change from previous year
India	79,736	up 6.9%
China	61,765	down 4.6%
Korea	52,484	up 1.9%
Japan	40,835	down 11.2%
Canada	27,017	up 1.9%
Taiwan	26,178	down 6.6%
Pakistan	7,325	down 9.8%

Like most immigrants, Asian Indians also came to America thinking that within a few years after they earned enough money or accomplished whatever else brought them to America, they would return back to their homeland. But as the years went by, more and more stayed on, which is known as 'X=X+1' syndrome – repeated postponement of return to India by one more year. As early as 1910, according to US immigration report, only 46 percent of the Asian Indians interviewed expressed an intention to return to India.[23] As they did not fully feel at home in America, they lived with the nostalgia of the past and always attempted to re-create the old world in their adopted world.

Like newcomers everywhere, they faced many hardships such as, minority complex, prejudice and discrimination. Nevertheless, many did excel in their adopted homeland and realized the American dream as they kept close ties with folks back home. They took occasional trips to visit their aging parents and other relatives. But more selfishly, many of the trips were intended to expose their children to the rich cultural and religious heritage of India. They desire for their children to pick up "Indian-ways" of doing things and have a healthy appreciation for 'where we came from'. Often these trips included visit to cousins, "uncles and aunties", grandparents, pilgrimage to holy sites, and participating in religious ceremonies. Unfortunately the residual memory of the second generation teens after these India visits often remain negative such as dirty surroundings, bugs, heat, lack of conveniences and comfort. Only when they grow older, they are able to look beyond the discomfort to develop some sense of appreciation for the Indian culture. The overwhelming advantages and habits that America offered like better living conditions, educational opportunities for the immigrant generation and their children, a better environment to raise children and religious freedom far outweighs the privilege of being close to native home and family.

Emerging Generations: 1.5G to 3G

In order to preserve cultural identity for subsequent generations, there needs to be a critical mass who intentionally adhere to their heritage, values, and traditions. The first wave of immigrants were unsuccessful because of restricted immigration policy and intermarriage with locals. They also failed to develop political, cultural, or religious institutions to uphold their unique identity and preserve their own cultural moorings.

However, with the second wave immigrants, it was different. For them, bringing their spouse and children to America and living together as a family was a priority. The first generation of post-1965 immigrants lived as nuclear families in the urban centers and suburbs of America. They even sponsored their siblings and other close relatives to come to America, forming their own extended family culture. Some even brought their entire clan over to America. Among them were many minors – children of the migrant parents. The pre-teen children who came to America have been commonly referred to as 1.5 generation of Indian-Americans, for they neither belonged to the first generation nor to the second. This generation shows a unique culture of their own – while their teen years and beyond are shaped by Western culture, their early upbringing in Indian culture is clearly evident. In effect, the adults see them as Americans, but their peers see them as Indians.

Then there are those who came to America in their late teens and beyond. They exhibit strong cultural underpinnings of their roots and the Americanization process is slower. There are also those who came to America by virtue of marriage in their 20s and 30s. In the eighties and nineties, many single migrants returned to India to get married (arranged by families) or to find spouses from compatible ethnic, caste, or religious class. These folks have their own blended sense of identity.

The emerging generation also includes individuals of Indian origin who were born elsewhere. Not every young Indian looking face has similar migratory paths. There are many who were born in Gulf countries, African nations, Far East Asia, Western Europe, or Canada, but now find themselves in the United States. They exhibit a unique blend of culture and outlook on life. Others included in the emerging generations of Indians in America are those Indians who have married non-Indians. They could be first generation immigrants from India or their children. They show higher levels of cultural assimilation and a fused sense of identity.

Most second wave immigrants also have had children after coming to America, thus creating the truly American born Indian generation, often referred to as the second generation. The second generation population continued to grow significantly through 70's and 80's. As natural citizens by account of their birth, their numbers and influence remain under the radar of most demographical studies or institutions. The Indian American community is relatively young. Nearly two-thirds of the Indian American community is 35 years old or younger and almost one-fourth is below the age of 15. This makes youth-work extremely strategic in Indian American communities and churches. However, the lack of resources, vision and trained personnel makes this task enormously challenging.

And by the year 2000, many of the American-born Asian Indians have come to marriageable age and are having children of their own. Thus forming the third generation of Indians in America, whose parental culture and peer culture are more American than prior generations.

Although the immigrant generation is somewhat similar in their migration experience and socio-economic status, the emerging generations are extremely complex for analysis. The generational characteristics alone will not be sufficient to define them. It is very difficult to locate a homogenous group of Indians and we might have to turn other ways to define the emerging generation. Anyone who has taken a serious look at the second generation tribe is sure to find the multidimensional aspect of their personality, often stretching and defying standard frameworks in understanding them.

Ajai's comment is valuable here. He said, "For the younger generation, especially those born after the 80's, we no longer see India as the motherland and yet we do not want to give it up entirely." The emerging generation is also looking at India from a different perspective. A youthworker in New York once told me, "I visited my ancestral village in Punjab to see the grave of my grandfather. He was a freedom fighter for the Indian independance. It was the most inspiring trip I have ever made."

The exploration of ethnic identity is intensifying as a new generation comes along. "It is a generational thing," reminds Dr. Thomas, "the first generation of Indians were very traditional. They cleaved to the motherland and continued to live there, psychologically. The second generation lost the links because they desperately wanted to be American. Now you have a third generation, and there's been a revival of ethnicity." The increased business activity as a result of liberalization of Indian economic policies in the nineties have heightened the interest and admiration of its cultural heritage. Americans are outsourcing business to India, while Indians in America are insourcing culture from India. Thomas explained, "They need culture, some kind of historical consciousness, some sense of self." The emerging generations will show greater resoluteness and commitment to search for their ethnic roots.

With growing outsourcing of technology-enabled jobs to India and reduction in visa-based migration, the second generation's influence and size are bound to overshadow the Indian migrant community. According to some estimates, with over 25,000 teenagers in Chicago and over 40,000 in New York, this generation will be a definitive shaper of the Indian community and culture in America. The second generation has finally come-of-age. They are slowly and steadily taking over social and cultural institutions that their parents have established. They are even exploring non-

Chart 2: Indian-American Population by Age & Sex[24]

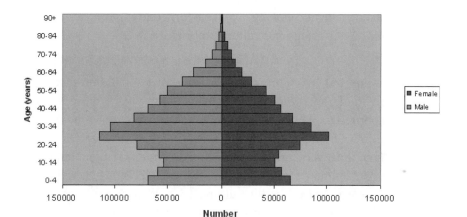

conventional fields , much against their parent's wishes like art, politics and media to assert their uniqueness and influence.

The immigrants of the late nineties are also different from their predecessors in that they were much more Americanized even as they arrived. The most recent immigrants have shown an entirely distinct culture in and of themselves. Having grown up with television and Internet, they were much exposed to the American culture and exhibit varying degrees of assimilation. These 20-somethings are much more comfortable with American ways and the balancing act between two ways of life. They have studied and worked in multi-ethnic and multicultural environments. They are globally aware, materialistic and liberal.

Having lived in cosmopolitan cities, many have interfaced with the American ethos even before ever landing here. They might even have an American accent, be familiar with the latest fashion, movie and music, dating college mates without their parent's knowledge, sexually active as singles, given up on religious matters, or having lived independently for a few years. Of course, not all will fit into this category. After seeing the American way of life, some young technology pros have turned to explore meaning in their own religious and cultural upbringings.

Thus, the Coconut generation cannot be solely defined by generation but by culture as well. Some of the children of the Indian immigrants who arrived here in their pre-teens, those who were born in the US, or some of those who arrived a few months to the college campuses show high levels of Americanization. At the same time, very few who were born in America still maintain strong inclination towards Indian culture. Though generation is a strong indicative of the culture, I would posit the broader subculture as the prime consideration in the writing about a generation. This project aims to locate Christian ministry issues with Americanized Asian Indians from a variety of immigrant experiences.

Coconut Dilemma: Caught in a Fix

A frequent question that the Coconut generation often gets asked in college and in the workplace is, "Where do you come from?" Sometimes they are mistaken for people from Pakistan, Sri Lanka or Bangladesh. In some instances, people from the North East Indian states like Nagaland or Mizoram are labeled as Chinese or even Korean. Because of their complex nature of self, they are often misunderstood by Indians as Americans and by Americans as Indian. As a result, they neither belong here nor there, often creating an inner conflict beyond their own understanding or people around them.

Another question Indians get asked in America is, "where did you learn to speak English?" They tend to compare Indians with other Asian immigrants who communicate mostly in their own mother tongues, but most Americans are unaware of the fact that India is a land of many languages and most Indians are able to understand or speak three or more languages. Believe it or not, more people in India communicate in English than the entire population of North America! It was the legacy of the British colonial rule and turned out to be the biggest advantage for Indians in its spread worldwide and has helped Indians to thrive in the technological industries. The language skill is a problematic area for the Coconut generation, who do not speak any other language other than English and speak it with a tinge of American accent. This creates more room for misunderstanding by Indians and Americans.

As early as 1945, Dr. S. Chandrasekar, a lecturer in Oriental Studies at the University of Pennsylvannia surveyed the Asian Indian community in America (first wave of immigrants) and remarked, "the improvement of their economic status was accompanied by the "Americanization" of their children. While the parents spoke Hindustani in the home, their children had begun to attend the local public schools and learned to speak English. For the American-born generation, India was "unreal and far away." But whether they were first or second generation Asian Indians, they felt isolated, not knowing for certain their place and future in America. In their identity, they seemed to be rooted neither here in America nor there in India. Some would like to go to India, marry and return to their adopted land; some would like relatives in India to come here and share the American way of life," explained Chandrasekar. But their cultural ties to India had been "cut asunder" and "new blood" from the homeland could not be introduced.[25]

Coconut existence is a series of painful adjustments and constant juggling of two worlds. The language predicament, academic difficulties, alienation from American peers, perceptions based on skin color, lack of confidence, need for affirmation, parental expectations, cultural and religious norms, finding friends, making career choices, finding love or a spouse, a God worth following, and being part of a faith community makes the Coconut life extremely challenging. Yet these experiences differentiate them from the rest of their kind.

Immigrant adults who want to help Coconuts face their own dilemma. Whether you are a parent of a Coconut or older brother/ sister, or a youth leader or a pastor, I believe adults have a key role in making this transitionary life stage easier for the Coconuts. In fact, Coconuts are looking for meaningful relationships with adults in order to make the move into the adult world. But the zeal to help, without knowledge of what they are really going through, could potentially do more harm than good. Some adults seem to detach helplessly, which is often interpreted as 'adults who don't care'. Others go to the opposite extreme and excessively interfere in the lives of Coconuts, resulting in young people loosing respect for the adults, rejecting their values, and ultimately swinging wildly towards radical narcissism.

Coconut Paradox: Best of Both or Worst of Both

Given the wide range of options before them, how do Coconuts view their future in America? Surprisingly the majority of Coconuts are becoming wary of the great American institutions. First, the economy does not hold the same promises it did for their parents. Continuing recession, growing national debt, rising unemployment figures, escalating housing costs etc. are disheartening this generation. Their parent's generation found a niche and were much more motivated to establish themselves in a strange land than the next. Even good education has become unaffordable for most Coconuts. The average cost annually for four-year college in 1970 was $9000, in 1990 it became $16,000, and in 2000 it rose to $30,000. Many Coconuts are forced to take excessive loans to pursue their professional studies. Others settle for community colleges or dropout to pursue other livelihoods. Then at the end of it all, the Coconuts are left with McJobs to pay off their student loans. Due to the recent trend in outsourcing knowledge-based jobs to India, they even feel cheated that their contemporaries in India are taking away many of their opportunities. When their cousins are becoming millionaires in India and keeping far better lifestyles, they wonder what is the big deal of growing up in America?

Second, the political system does not seem to hold any promise. Like most of the migrant communities, the Indians favored political parties that were interested in meeting their immediate needs, pursuing their aspirations and advancing their welfare. But the Coconut generation without immigrant needs, expectations, undefined personal values and convictions are in limbo with regard to their political affiliation. Few Coconuts are politically savvy, while most are staying out of it altogether.

Third, the family, the great conventional social institution that America took pride in is disintegrating. The sexual revolution of the 60s and the lack of moral leadership resulted in broken marriages, unwanted pregnancies, and incurable diseases causing much pain in families all across the nation. Coming from a more family-centered kinship culture, the first generation of Indians were very protective of their offspring from the family fallout of the mainstream society. However, what parents failed to show to their kids was that they were happily married and enjoyed each other. Even though the Coconuts did not see much divorce among their parents' generation, they witnessed mundane and less desirable marriages. It seemed to them that their parents simply lived together for the sake of children and/or the fear of social ostracization. As a result of demanding careers and scheduling conflicts, the parents had very limited meaningful communication with their children. Though few Coconuts have made best of both worlds, the large percentage view their future less optimistically.

Roots, Shoots, or Fruits: What to Pursue?

What is rooted-ness? And why is it important in our self discovery? Most people grow up oblivious of their ancestry. In many parts of India, families preserve their family history. A few years ago, I attended our annual *'kudubha yogam'* (family gathering). There I met our family historian for the first time, who helped me to trace back my ancestry over a few centuries. The family records had many details of who my forefathers married, where they lived, and children they bore. I drew a family tree from the information I had collected. It was my quest for my own roots.

> Remember, your aren't feeding the root,
> the root is feeding you.
> Rom 11:18 (Message)

For the immigrant generation of St. Thomas Christians, one of the introductory question (after finding out their name) is often, "what is your family or house name?" That will tell everything about yourself. Individuals are known by their forefathers. Family names describe their ethnic purity, wealth, education and status in the society. Some took pride in their Syrian lineage, others took pride in their forefathers who were among the early Christians, and others took pride in descending from well-known community leaders. When marriage alliances are brought, people closely scrutinized pedigree. Until a generation or two ago, who you were was defined by where you came from. Ancestry seemed to define one's destiny. Your education, skills, wealth or accomplishments mattered very little.

In the Indian culture, like that in Old Testament, names meant a great deal. It was more than mere identification. Names are often an accurate description of the person or their chief characteristics. Also, many names were mentioned as 'son of so and so'. Ancestry was important, and your profession was closely linked to the caste you belonged to. The caste system and social hierarchy of ancient India (higher priestly caste still use it to oppress the majority lower caste) are still prevalent in many parts of India today.

Some Coconuts deny their ethnic roots vehemently. They think, "We are now in America. Why bother about India? I want to break free from the cultural baggage and the bondage of the past. I want to be known for who I am and what I do with my life now, not what I have inherited – color of skin and ethnicity. I had no choice in those matters." In fact, many of these Coconuts view Indian ways as archaic and burdensome and harbor negative feelings towards them. For them, shoots is all that matters. "Who cares about roots? After all they are under the ground? What is seen is what really matters."

Important as they are - roots or shoots, Jesus also taught that a tree is known by its fruits (Matthew 12:23). We name a tree by the fruit it produces. So what I do with life and what others receive from me, will define who I am. What we produce is a result of who we are and significantly influenced by where we come from. Although we did not have any say in where we were born, we can choose to ignore or chose to learn about our historic past.

Every aspect of our lives – roots, shoots and fruits are important. In some aspects of our lives we may have a choice, but most others we have none. Some things are done to us without our consent or knowledge. We should strive to make the most of all that is offered to us instead of picking on the worst that comes our way.

Why Does it All Matters?

The roots of our ethnicity, routes of our migration, shoots of our American education and fruits of our destiny are all closely tied together. It is easy to deny or ignore some of these factors that constitute an irrefutable part of us. In fact, when we turn a blind eye to some of these aspects of our existence, something within us dies. And with the rest, life seems incomplete. If we fail to learn lessons from history, we are bound to repeat its mistakes. The stories of struggle and survival of the immigrants are source of tremendous inspiration and can propel us into our future.

To understand the present, it is necessary to understand the past. To learn how we got where we are, we must trace backwards. That is precisely why I briefly tried to map the Indian migration in this chapter in order to develop greater understanding of the coconut generation. Our rootedness secures us like an anchor of a ship in a turbulent sea. Moreover, in chaotic times like ours, we want to anchor on to things that are not affected by the winds and storms of life. An anchor is only as good as the object it anchors on to. The seabed is unmoved by the storms on the surface and provides stability to the ship amidst the wildest tempest. Doesn't the foundation of a building determine the size and strength of its superstructures? What lies beneath the ground and cannot be seen shapes what lies above the ground.

In its heart of hearts, the Coconut generation does not want to fully assimilate into its host environment to become pure "American". Their Indian-ness not only gives them a unique identity, but also provides a rootedness. It is noticeable that the majority of them in their teen years try to distance themselves from everything Indian, yet in later years they become increasingly curious about their Indianness. They begin to embrace their bi-cultural uniqueness and celebrate their "twoness". There is no clash between the cultures, but they welcome the fusion of the East and the West, budding into an entirely new self. The Coconut generation stands on the borderline that separated their two different worlds and becomes a bridge across the wide chasm. Two stream of rivers - the great Indian civilization with all its heritage and the American civilization with its scientific advancements, merges in the Coconut generation to form a giant river.

More than all human lineage and manmade social structures, we need to find our rootedness in God as our creator. If we dare to trace our origin all the way back, we will arrive at God – the creator of all. The very beginning of our existence originated in the mind of God. Therefore, I am not an accident, nor am I result of mere careful planning by my parents. It was God who knit me together in my mother's womb (Psalm 139:13). Not only did God create me, but he loves and made provision for me to enjoy fellowship with him and has wonderful plans concerning my life (John 10:10, Jeremiah 29:11). This awareness is very liberating and frees me from socio-cultural and psychological bondage. God alone can re-center me, bring life in focus and help me discover the purpose for which I was created. My past need not limit my future. God wipes my slate clean and gives me a fresh start in life to explore all it is worth and to actualize its full potential. God alone can heal all my hurts, failures and struggles. Yet with God's help, I can fully celebrate the roots of my ethnicity and routes of my life's journeys.

To Ponder About:

1. Trace your roots and draw a family tree with dates, locations and people.

2. Interview your parents and other first generation individuals to hear their stories of immigration.

3. How much does roots of your ethnicity or routes of your imigration shape who you are?

4. What are the strengths and weaknesses of roots and routes in identity formation?

5. Research second generation population in your school, neighborhood, state etc. and list identity shaping influences on them.

Endnotes

[1] Popular song in a Bollywood classic, *Sri 420*.

[2] http://www.time.com/time/asia/2003/journey/story.html (accessed Mar 25, 2005)

[3] www.census.gov/population/www/socdemo/foreign.html (accessed Mar 25, 2005)

[4] Government of India – Ministry of External Affairs, Report on Indian Diaspora, Dec 2001. (www.Indiaday.com/government_policy/singhavi2.asp (accessed Mar 25, 2005)

[5] For more on global Indian Diaspora and its history, see books mentioned in the bibliography. Also visit www.coconutgeneration.com for data and links.

[6] US Census Bureau, The Asian Population 2000.

[7] Vinay Lal, A Potential History of Asian Indians in America, Leela Prasad ed., *Live Like the Banyan Tree: Images of the Indian American Experience* (Philadelphia: Balch Institute for Ethnic Studies, 1999) 42-44.

[8] LEAP (Leadership Education for Asian Pacifics). 1993. *The State of Asian Pacific America: Policy Issues to the Year 2020.* Los Angeles: UCLA Asian American Studies Center and Asian Pacific American Public Policy Institute.

[9] US Census Bureau, Census 2000. www.census.gov/population/www/socdemo/foreign.html (accessed Feb 23, 2005)

[10] Adapted from Urmila Minocha, "South Asian Immigrants: Trends and Impacts on the Sending and Receiving Societies," in *Pacific Bridges: The New Immigration from Asian and the Pacific Islands,* James T Fawcett and Benjamin V. Carino eds. (New York: Center for Migration Studies, 1987) 348. *Statistical Year Book 2000* from INS (Washing ton DC: US Government Printing Office). Also online at http://uscis.gov/graphics/shared/statistics/yearbook/2000/imm2000list.htm (accessed Mar 25, 2005)

[11] Hindi slang meaning 'Let's go to America'

[12] Ronald Takaki, *Strangers from a Different Shore: A History of Asian Americans,* (New York: Penguin Books, 1989) 294.

[13] Most of these data taken from Census report , "We the people – Asians in the US" from www.census.gov dated Dec 2004.

[14] Timothy Fong, *The Contemporary Asian American Experience: Beyond the*

Model Minority (Englewood Cliff, NJ: Prentice Hall, 2002) 73.

[15] US Census Bureau, Census 2000 Sample File 2.

[16] Paul M. Ong, Lucie Cheng, and Leslie Evans, "Migration of Highly Educated Asians and Global Dynamics," *Asian and Pacific Migration Journal,* Vol. 1, Nos. 3-4 (1992), 545.

[17] Figure 9 of "We the People report on Asians in the US", Census 2000. Issued Dec 2004.

[18] Figure 12 of "We the People report on Asians in US", Census 2000. Issued Dec 2004.

[19] Karen Isaksen Leonard, *The South Asian Americans,* (Connecticut: Greenwood Press, 1997) 69.

[20] James P. Streba, "Indians in US Prosper in their New Country, and not just in Motels," *Wall Street Journal,* January 27, 1987.

[21] E.M. Wherry, "Hindu Immigrants in America," in *Missionary Review of the World,* Vol. 30 (December 1907), 918-919.

[22] US Institute of International Education's Open Doors 2004 Survey Report.

[23] Ronald Takaki, *Strangers from a Different Shore: A History of Asian Americans,* (New York: Penguin Books, 1989) 308.

[24] See Appendix A2 for age-based population and gender ratio.

[25] Ronald Takaki, *Strangers from a Different Shore: A History of Asian Americans,* (New York: Penguin Books, 1989) 314.

3

Evolving Identity:
Self-Concept of Coconuts

Thou hast made us for thyself, O Lord, and
our hearts are restless until they find their rest in thee.
— St. Augustine

Ask any teenager, "who are you?" they may reply "I am so and so (his or her name)". They will try to get away with a quick answer. But if you are like me, I tend to prod the enquiry a little further. "Who are you, really? What defines you? What is inside of you? What will best describe you fully?" I know that this interrogation can be pretty overwhelming and even intimidating. I also know that many have struggled to answer these questions and they haven't articulated their thoughts or feelings in any concrete manner. Believe me I do not do that to every teenager I come across. But I have tried with people that I have known for a while and got many interesting and insightful answers.

For example, take Tom's case. Tom is a nineteen-year-old young man, American-born Indian, a committed Christian, grew up in Los Angeles; in college pursuing a degree in computers and education; his parents are from Chennai and grandparents came from Kottayam, Kerala; he is the only child of his parents; who wanted him to be a doctor; he is single and is dating a Caucasian girl, whom he met in college; he is somewhat active in the Christian campus fellowship and a local church; serves as volunteer in an environmental group; owns a pet dog; works part time at the campus library. The list goes on.

None of these by itself will define Tom completely. Every detail is important and helps us paint a more complete picture of who Tom really is. In some cases, not all the pieces can be glued together and consistent with the rest. Some pieces may only be loosely attached, but they help us understand him a little better. Yet, his real inner self is beyond all these external manifestations.

So what really defines us? We are back to the age old question – "Who am I?" Conventional wisdom tells us is that it is during the teen years that this quest is most pronounced. Am I what my parents try to make me to be, or what others see me as, or is it my inner self, or is it a gift from God? What sort of a person am I? Developmental psychology has taught us that if we gain nothing else from adolescence, we must obtain a coherent sense of self (identity) to navigate future life stages successfully.

Identity: Who Am I?

Young people grow up quickly into adult bodies, but socially, intellectually, and emotionally they are not yet ready to carry out responsibilities of adult self. In some cases, teenagers themselves do not fully understand the crises in their lives any better than do the adults around them. This crisis can best be phrased as questions that teens attempt to answer – "Who am I?" or "What do other people think about me?"

> **"Who am I, and who are my people ..."**
> **1 Chronicles 29:14 (NIV)**

48

Moving to a new country and adjusting to the new world is often the major cause of stress to first generation immigrants. But their progeny have to grapple with the psychological and social dilemma of their self discovery. "Adults tend to treat adolescents as "big kids" or "little adults". They are neither. Yet they are both."[1] Most Indian American youth feel torn between being Indian and being American, a predicament shaped by their Indian upbringing and American socialization. Having grown up in a homogenized culture back in India, the first generation is often unaware and insensitive to the struggle of the second generation in discovering their identities in a new land.

The development of an Americanized identity is countered by the concomitant pull of the ethnic identity. The ethnic identity is shaped by the harsh reality of racism which may lead one to reject or enhance his or her ethnic identity. The skin color, languages, stereotypes etc only make things difficult for the second generation. Compared to their parents, they often become much more assimilated into the dominant society and thus have less ethnic identification. However, the consciousness, adoption, and application of the ethnic identity will ebb and flow depending on one's life experiences. A person may choose to adopt only certain aspects of ethnicity or to invoke the identity only in certain settings like at home but not at school or work. Furthermore, a person who 'lives in a predominantly ethnic neighborhood would most likely invoke his identity more often than one who lives in a white-dominated area.'[2]

The formation of independent selfhood is one of the very important tasks that they must set for themselves. A great deal of a person's identity formation takes place during adolescence. During that period most young people discover a personal anchor point in an inner self-identity. Identity is a result of the distinction from the "other" and the internalization of the relationship to

49

the other; it arises out of the complex history of differentiation in which both the self and the other take part by negotiating their identities in interaction with one another[3].

East vs West: Differing Notions of Identity

Before we get any further, at this juncture, I feel it would be appropriate to understand a couple of theoretical frameworks that lie beneath the identity forming issues among Indian-Americans. One is American and the other is Indian, both of whom are widely accepted for their significant contributions to this field.

During the 1950s and 60s, Psychologist Erik Erikson posited a psychosocial approach to understanding identity by describing the interplay between the individual biology, psychology and social recognition and response within an historical context. He suggested that to be fully mature, an individual has to have a sense of ego identity, an idea or set of ideas of ourselves that is enduring and continuous over time. "[Ego Identity's] most obvious concomitants are a feeling of being at home in one's body, a sense of 'knowing where one is going', and an inner assuredness of anticipated recognition from those who count."[4] According to Erikson, there is personal identity, consisting of one's values and aspirations and a social identity deriving from the many roles one may play in life, for example as son/daughter, brother/sister, friend, sportsperson, employee, father/mother, or husband/wife.

Erikson suggested that mature identity is achieved through a process of exploration and experimentation during teen years. Some adolescents make up their minds too quickly and achieve an identity that doesn't suit their personalities, which is labeled the 'identity foreclosure'. Some others alternatively, might never arrive from their period of exploration and drift forever uncertain of their identity, which is labeled the 'identity diffusion'.

Some of the key concepts that he introduced to us are: the chief characteristic of the teen years is their *identity crisis*. Erikson viewed a *psychological moratorium* to be an important developmental process in which young adults freely experiment with various possible adult roles in order to find one that seems to provide a unique fit.[5] Another important concept was *Identity vs Role confusion* – the fifth of the eight stage human developmental theory that comes to the fore during adolescence.

In the 1970s, Indian Psychologist Sudhir Kakar postulated a different approach from Erikson to understand identity development in the Indian society. According to him, many of the salient aspects of the Indian society like family-centeredness, religion, regional affiliation, language, caste/class, etc. plays a crucial role in the development of the self concept. An individual self is seen within a communal self; individual accomplishments are valued only if it improves the well being and/or status of one's family or community. The guiding principle is that the collective identity affirms preservation and enhancement of the well being of the group, rather than individual identity of any member of that group. Every person of a group is expected to uphold the collective identity over individual identity; even expected to subjugate their own inclinations and make personal sacrifices, if needed. In conflictual situations, everyone always regards their collective self over their personal self.

Caste and gender further accentuates the issue of identity development in Indian society. As Kakar points out, "the daughter in a Hindu family hardly ever develop an identity of her own. She is expected to remain chaste and pure and upon reaching marriageable age, she is seen as economic liability because of dowry. On entering her married home, her status changes. She is seen as a wife, as a daughter-in-law, as a sister-in-law in the new home. And then as a mother, a grandmother and should her husband predeceases her, as a widow. In the new home, she burys her past and new identity is ascribed to her. No permanent identity, but ever changing identity from her changing role." [6]

Identity is less achieved and more ascribed; ascribed by birth, family, community, caste, status, religion, etc. The ascribed identity tends to restrict choices open to the individual. According to this notion, one's identity to a large extent tends to be the reflection of familial and social norms and expectations. Personal interests, goals, welfare, and glory is secondary to that of the family. In order to attain harmony within the family, it is essential for an individual to surrender or merge into his or her family, resulting in the loss of his or her individuality.

In the West, the development of the individual identity is generally seen in socio-psycho-sexual-cognitive terms (Erikson, Freud, Piaget). The West values individualism, independence and innovation, while the Eastern societies value community, interdependence and tradition. In Eastern cultures like India, development of identity has a strong bearing on the surrounding community. Erik Erikson suggests that every culture devises ways for its young people to take a moratorium in ways that are keeping with the society's values. Some will avoid the challenge of self definition by following the traditional socialization pathways historically offered by the culture as represented in their local community. For ethnic minority groups living within majority cultures, as is the case for Coconut generation, awareness of their cultural ancestry is vital to their sense of ego identity much more than their Caucasian peers.

> **I see you seeing me:**
> **I see the me you think you see.**
> **You see you according to me:**
> **You see the you think I see.**
> **James Fowler**

Perception Matters: Who Do People Say that I Am

Psychology tells us that we form our identities through the eyes of other people. The people surrounding us play a crucial role in how we form our self concept. How they approve or disapprove, accept or reject, reinforce or undermine plays a vital role in the development of my ego identity. These people could be parents, siblings, friends, media, etc. They help paint the ideal self and create motivations to emulate that ideal self.

Anjali is a second generation Indian who grew up in one of the few Indian families in the suburbs of Connecticut and her only contact with other Indians was through the community church in New York that the family visited once a month. Her primary contacts, especially close friends, were Caucasians. For her, culture shock was the large number of Indian-Americans at New York University. She now has an Indian American boyfriend, even though her behavior and expectations seems more "American" than "Indian-American."

Another second generation Indian, Manju grew up in a predominantly Indian neighborhood of Edison, New Jersey. She is bilingual and well versed in Indian cultural aspects. She was surrounded by Indian-Americans while growing up and she was somewhat isolated from other cultures. For her, culture shock was enrolling at the same NYU campus as Anjali, where everyone was not of Indian origin!

Most Americans view India as a 'Hindu' nation and consider all Indian immigrants as followers of the Hindu religion. They are ignorant of the fact that India has been multi-religious for many centuries. There are many adherents of Islam, in fact the second largest Islamic population in the world is in India. India is also the birth place of Bhuddism, Jainism, and Sikhism. Christianity existed in India since the first century A.D. It is believed that

Apostle Thomas, one of the twelve disciples of Jesus, brought the gospel to the southern coast of India in A.D. 52. In fact, many centuries before America was even discovered or Christianity reached Europe, there was a faithful community of Christ-followers in India.

Similarly, most Indians view Western culture as morally liberal and fear that their children will not keep the conservative values that they have grown up with. Some even associate permissive culture with Christianity and tend to isolate themselves in order to preserve their children from the corruption of the West.

The need for relationship is paramount as youths navigate through adolescence. The young adolescents are always looking for another person who really serves as a projection of their idealized self. The mirroring process is necessary in identity formation and also makes them vulnerable to peer pressure. Since no single reflection of self is accurate, youths will seek many friends in order to gain the benefit of multiple reflections.

In her recent book – *Practicing Passion,* Kenda Creasy Dean calls the church to be passionate with young people. She writes,

> Every adolescent longs for a center that holds, a sacred core to the fractured soul. Passion reveals the human desire to construct a self in relationship to a reliable "other" – just as passion revealed God's desire to show the divine self in relationship to us in Jesus Christ. Our identities take shape in relationship that mirror back to us "who we are" and the kind of person we are becoming, but not just any relationship will do. Ultimately, identity requires the self-confirming presence of reliable love. The intuition that we can be "loved into being" by other impels us to keep looking for this reliable love, even when lesser love disappoint. And when we do find it, this authentic love reorders our view of the world and our place in it.[7]

As important as human mirrors are to define our identity, it is fundamental to know how God sees us. For God alone is self existent, self sufficient and needs nothing else to define the divine self. Who we are in God's eyes is of utmost importance in identity formation; for God alone can reflect who we truly are. Our spiritual identity has power to transform all other identities from the inside out, far beyond the distorted reflections of peers, parents, role models and other significant adults.

Minority Complex: Double Marginalization

A common self-perception of all immigrants is that they are minorities. The majority is what matters in a secular democratic society and it determines the place of minorities within. If minority syndrome is bad, the second generation exhibits double minority syndrome. They suffer from double marginalization - first on account of their ethnicity, and secondly due to generational differences. They become a minority within a minority in the multiethnic, multicultural world of the United States.

The term 'model minority' was coined in 1966 by sociologist William Peterson to describe Japanese Americans. Since then it has been applied to other immigrants when American media noticed the great success of many Asian Americans like the *Newsweek* headline "The Asian-Americans: the model minority"[8]. And since the 90s, Asian-Indians have been called the model minority, largely due to success stories of Indians in professional fields and business. Both education and income levels are the highest in the country. Although model minority may be taken as a compliment, such generalization is unfair for diverse group of people. This myth might do more harm than good: overlook less educated and less affluent immigrants, create resentment in non-Indians within American society, (as was evident at the debate on outsourcing software contracts to India) and promote discriminatory policies and practices.

The model minority syndrome also negatively affects the emerging generations. It sets both unrealistic expectation and artificial precedents to emulate. This only aggravates the unpleasant tension between the generations. Furthermore, the inability to handle failure and the unattainable goals prescribed by parents and community increases the pain of failure. This results in perpetual conflicts, extreme rebellion, physical abuse, running away from home and in some cases teenage suicides.

Coconut Identity: WIP (Work-In-Progress)

In early childhood, the Indian-American generation is more inclined toward Indian ways, but all that changes drastically as they begin daycare or schooling. Through adolescence, most lean toward embracing the American side of their identity and tend to distance themselves from their parent's way of doing things. When they move into adulthood and enter the workforce, they experience the weight of racial prejudice. For some second generation, identification with the Indian culture stems from their marginalized status in the pluralistic world. For others, the quest for their Indian-ness and meaning of religious/cultural practices aids their self discovery.

Another major confusion that prevails in this life stage concerns morality. Having observed physical changes in their bodies, they now strongly feel sexual urges and are naturally drawn to people of the opposite sex. This developmental issue gets further aggravated for young people growing in a sexually permissive culture where media is constantly bombards them with liberal alternatives. The Eastern value system is more consistent with

Christian values when it comes to family, morality, and education. This creates further confusion in the minds of Coconut generation and their parents. Amidst all this prevailing confusion, they are looking for moral guidelines and trustworthy adults who can steer them through this quagmire of moral choices.

An individual's language and culture is not inherited through biological transmission or genetics. One acquires his or her language and culture through enculturation, by learning the language and various symbols, values, norms and beliefs in the environment to which one is exposed. The term 'ethnicity' has come to define an individual's cultural heritage and marked distinctively from one's physical characteristics. The objective ethnicity includes observable culture and shared symbols of a particular group, while subjective ethnicity involves internal beliefs of the people regarding their shared ancestry. The examples of objective ethnicity are clothing, food, language, and religious traditions while subjective aspects of the ethnicity entails a 'we-feeling' or a sense of community. It distinguishes the 'my world' from 'their world'. This subjective identification of individuals is based on an ideology of a shared history, unique past, symbolic attachments to homeland and other commonality of experiences that play an important role in defining one's identity.

It was always a question of allegiance, "I wanted to please my parents and meet their expectations. I also wanted to meet the expectations of my American peers, and the expectations I put on myself to fit into American society." It's a classic case of divided identity, but depending on the degree to which the immigrants in question are willing to assimilate, the conflict is more or less pronounced. The increased experimentation in risky behaviors like drugs, reckless driving, sex, and violence may serve to distract them from overwhelming internal conflicts. Theologian Loder warned us of the problem, "The greater danger to the human spirit in this is not from adolescent but from sociocultural side: the fear of nonconformity on the part of the status quo society will not so much redirect or transform the human spirit, but if possible, suppress or break it so it will conform without complaint."[9]

The "achieved" notion of identity according to the Western understanding and the "ascribed" notion of identity according to the Eastern understanding perfectly converge in Coconut generation, creating a pull in opposite directions, tearing the soul of this generation. The tension is most acute within the members of second generation than any other in the ethnic communities.

Evolving Identity: New ID.

In spite of the fact that Erikson's theory of identity is widely accepted, it is not without its critics. His understanding of the task of identity formation exclusively in the adolescent years is questionable. In fact, identity development begins in the early years of life and continues throughout one's life; it does not begin and end in adolescence as Erikson suggested. With a plethora of new options ever before us, the exploration never really ends. The transitionary nature of post-modern life stages are evident due to changing economic pressures, changing nature of work/leisure, divorce and remarriage, travel etc.

More recent scholarship on identity development has challenged the traditional view of coherent self concept during adolescent years. Friedrich Shcweitzer tells us that 'identity formation turns out to be a flexible and a lifelong process. As the experience of transitional periods in life has multiplied, the need to re-work and to re-establish one's identity has also become an enduring task never to be quite completed."[10] Teen years may be when identity crisis is most acute, but is by no means 'the time of life when personal identity is developed and established once and for all.'[11]

The identity formation cannot be taken in isolation and Eastern understanding of identity in kinship cultures have helped to develop a relational, interdependent self concept. Ascribed identity is equally important as achieved identity and the community impact cannot be overlooked anymore in the identity formation process. Realistically, a firm and fixed autonomous independent self can never be achieved. For women, Erikson's model of identity has challenged ideal visions of the autonomous and independent self and has been considered distortive and oppressive.[12] For most women, personal identity involves not just meeting one's own needs, but also responding to the needs of the others; they tend to form identity in the relational context.

The sociologist Peter Berger called modern man "homeless" and in a state of "permanent identity crisis." According to Berger, "Modern consciousness entails a movement from fate to choice …Roles no longer actualize the self, but serve as a "veil of *maya*" hiding the self not only from others but also from the individuals own consciousness. Only in the interstitial areas left vacant by institutions … can the individual hope to discover or define himself."[13]

Fragmented self has become a contemporary reality. Identity is no more a single, fixed self description and fully developed during any particular phase of life. But it is ever evolving and constantly changing. Plural Self and plural identities are the new concepts to describe this new notion of self definition. Also identity is related to social norms and cultural bearings within a community. The inner self and spirituality have also come to shape postmodern concept of identity.

Identity integration is key to holding together multiple identities, even if they seem opposing or contradictory. The "braids" of multiple identities are woven together to form the whole and the whole seems to be larger than the sum total of its parts. The integration of various unique identities is a greater work than discovernig individual strands. Integration can be seen as moving beyond mono or stereo sounds to develop a polyphonic sensibility; an ability to harmonize the music of orchestra.

But not all Coconuts want to integrate everything; they are comfortable with discrete pieces of their identities. No single identity is able to define them completely. They constantly wrestle to hold on to every identity simultaneously. The postmodern culture requires multiple identities depending on the situation and people involved. Coconuts adapt like a chameleon to multiple roles and circumstances. This generation is learning the art of jugglery and has become experts in juggling multiple identities. At any given point in time, some of their identities are in the air! They may have to throw what is in their hand into the air in order to catch other 'identities' that are coming down. As they grow older, more identities get thrown into the juggling act and they have to throw them higher. When they miss some, they crash land on the ground. Some are able to keep more 'identities' in the air than others can. Only in the beginning and at the end of our life, do we have all the "identities" in our hands!

Christian Identity: A Gift

Most religious youth programs aim to serve two purposes: to help youths navigate safe passage into adulthood and to offer both faith and cultural identities. In many ethnic communities faith and cultural identities are so intertwined that they appear one and the same. Biblical Christianity demands Christian youthwork to help their constituents establish their personal identity in Christ. At the core of this identity lies an all encompassing change of loyalty, from a given culture with its gods to the God of all cultures.[14] What is particularly Christian about one's identity is that it underscores "inherent relationality of human identity, which is revealed only in relationship to God and others; true identity is ours by redemption, not by human development. The Christian identity requires a differentiated ego, not an autonomous one, the humility to recognize and value the other as other. Christian theology challenges Erickson's concept of identity "achievement" by proclaiming true humanity as God's gift, obscured by sin but restored by Christ."[15]

The God's salvific act in Jesus Christ has a profound way of renewing and re-centering the self. Christ enables us to make all things anew, "if any man be in Christ, he is a new creature: old things are passed away; behold, all things are become new." (2 Cor 5:17) Jurgen Moltmann claims that, "Christian identity can be understood only as an act of identification with the Crucified Christ."[16] For Christians, the identity is a gracious gift and not something that you work for or seek after. While that identity is distorted by sin, Jesus restored our relationship with God; and he made visible once more our identities as God's beloved. Then our identity is rooted in the doctrine of creation and redemption. Theologian Mirosalv Volf put it as – Christian Identity takes shape in the midst of both belief-shaping practices and practice-shaped beliefs.[17]

Who we really are changes with the context; our true identity can be seen as a shifting shadow. The danger of relativism, pluralism and compartmentalization is real with plural self. "Although Christian tradition supports the plural self's contexuality, brokenness and even a normative partialness, it does not support its relativism: when everything matters, nothing matters most. ..to have integrity, the plural self requires a theologically compelling center to which the self's plurality can cling, a core that remains faithful and true."[18]

The shape of my shadow is determined by the angle of the lights, brightness, obstructions, and other things around me. It is constantly changing with my every move and changes with any of the other factors. Not everything is within my control nor can I determine how my shadow will look. Just as the greatest shadow forming force is the light from the sun, likewise our changing identity will never be fully comprehended unless we take an honest look at the Light of the world – Jesus Christ and establish a vibrant, dynamic relationship with him.

The Coconut adolescence is a time of both promise and peril. If it turns out well, young people can find an enduring sense of identity, purpose and faith through fidelity to a vision of the self they are called to be. If it does not, it leaves behind much pain and disillusionment, not just for the individual but for the entire community.

To Ponder About:

1. What are some painful and pleasant memories of what other people said about your skin color or ethnicity?

2. How has your sense of self and other changed through childhood, preteen, teen and college years?

3. Recollect your early encounters with people unlike you?

4. How will you describe yourself and how has your self concept changed over the last three years?

5. List three people who have played a crucial role in shaping your identity? How?

Endnotes

[1] Richard Dunn & Mark Senter III, *Reaching a Generation for Christ,* (Chicago: Moody Press, 1997) 36.

[2] Uba Laura, *Asian Americans: Personality Patterns, Identity and Mental health,* (New York: Guildford Press, 1994) 89-118

[3] Miroslav Volf, *Exclusion & Embrace: A Theological Exploration of Identity, Otherness and Reconciliation,* (Nashville: Abingdon Press, 1996) 66.

[4] Eric Erikson, *Identity: Youth and Crisis,* (New York: W.W. Norton, 1965) 165.

[5] Ibid. 156.

[6] Sudhir Kakar, *The Inner World: A Psychoanalytic Study of Childhood and Society in India* (New Delhi: Oxford University Press, 1981)

[7] Kenda Creasy Dean, *Practicing Passion: Youth and the Quest for a Passionate Church,* (Grand Rapids: Eerdmans, 2004) 55-56.

[8] Newsweek, Dec 6, 1982, 39ff.

[9] James E. Loder, *The Logic of the Spirit: Human Development in Theological Perspective,* (California: Jossey Boss, 1998) 205.

[10] Fredrich Schweitzer, *Post Modern Life Cycle: The Challenge for Church and Theology,* (Atlanta: Chalice Press, 2004) 49.

[11] Philip Graham, *End of Adolescence,* (New York: Oxford University Press, 2004) 19.

[12] Carol Gilligan, *Different Voices: Psychological Theory and Women's Development,* (Boston: Harvard University Press, 1993).

[13] Peter Berger, *The Homeless Mind,* (New York: Random House, 1973) 93-94.

[14] Miroslav Volf, *Exclusion and Embrace: A Theological Exploration of Identity, Otherness and Reconciliation,* (Nashville: Abingdon Press, 1996) 40.

[15] Kenda Dean, *Practicing Passion: Youth and the Quest for a Passionate Church,* (Grand Rapids: Eerdmans, 2004) 84.

[16] Jurgen Moltmann, *The Crucified God,* (Minneapolis: Fortress Press, 1993) 19.

[17] Mirosalv Volf,"Theology for a Way of Life," in *Practicing Theology,* Miroslav Volf and Dorothy C. Bass eds., (Grand Rapids: Eerdmans, 2002) 250-251.

[18] Kenda Dean, *Practicing Passion: Youth and the Quest for a Passionate Church,* (Grand Rapids: Eerdmans, 2004) 87.

4

Authentic Hybrids:
Bi-Culturalism of Coconuts

East is East; West is West; and never the twain shall meet.
– Rudyard Kipling[1]

Kaka, the crow, did not like his feathers. "I wish I was a peacock!" he would say. "Kaka, you are beautiful as you are!" the other crows told him. "How plain and dull you all look to me!" Kaka would complain, and fly off to admire peacocks. The peacocks strutted about with their colorful tail feathers outstretched. To the delight of the crow, some of the peacock feathers lay on the ground when the peacocks left.

Kaka flew down to the ground and stuck the feathers into his wings and tail. He attached a few sticking up from his head. "Now I am as beautiful as a peacock," Kaka said. But, when he went to join them in their strutting, the peacocks poked him and pecked him. "You are not a peacock," they said and chased Kaka away.

Bruised and still dragging some broken peacock feathers in his tail, Kaka returned home. But the crows also rejected Kaka saying, "You look different, got colorful feathers. You are not one among us." Kaka had no friends. No one wanted his company! As Kaka sat alone, he realized, "It's foolish to try and be what you're not. I must learn to love the feathers I've got!"

Culture is like kaka's feathers and contemporary realities are not as black and white as it used to be. In the past, two diametrically opposite ideas could never come together, but more recently on account of unprecedented mixing up, the grey matter seems to have taken over the world. The emerging generation is exposed to a wide range of new hues and they are creating new shades of a masterpiece.

Culture is an important concept we must understand in order to gain access into the lives of the Coconut generation. Anthropologists use the term in a much broader sense to refer to all of the learned and shared ideas and products of a society. Broadly, the term "culture" could be defined as a shared way of life that includes values, beliefs, and norms transmitted within a particular society from generation to generation.[2] Culture thus consists of symbols, language, values, beliefs, worldviews, myths, ideologies and norms. Whenever two or more cultures come together, there is constant import and export of cultural expressions. As one group of people comes in contact with other groups of people, there is constant borrowing from each others culture. Over a period of time these import/export results in the evolution of entirely new cultural forms. Intermarriages, socio-political conditions, technology, economics etc are other factors shaping the emergence of new contemporary blended cultures.

Living in Two Worlds: Home & Abroad

The Coconuts often ask, not audibly but mentally, "Am I an Indian or am I an American?" They somehow cannot deny either part of their existence. There is a tension between their dual natures of their inner wiring. Their lives seem to be bifurcated between the land of their parents and the land of birth or adoption. They are pulled in one direction at home and another direction at school. They speak their ancestral language at home and English elsewhere. Their mothers put their younger siblings to sleep singing Indian lullabies, while they heard another kind of music at college dorms. "My parents sang old devotional songs in Malayalam at church," Abey told me, "but I preferred contemporary worship songs in English. Difference is not just the language, but genre of music."

The food habits of Coconut generation expose their inherent duality. At home they eat rice/roti and curries, but once they step outside the doors they prefer American food. Although many Coconuts like the Indian delicacies, they are not very keen to learn to make them. The 20-year old Aishwarya readily admitted, "Indian cooking is too complicated, I like eating them and not making them." Mixing things are more obvious in the world of fashion, music, art and cinema - wearing sari and business suits, eating roti and pasta, playing guitar with *sitar and tabala*, dancing *Bharat Natyam* and ballet etc. They blend the annual trips to their grandparents' homes with the dating rituals of an Ivy League school and the Bollywood music of their fathers' collection with the jazz beats of Manhattan's moon-lit bars. The East-West amalgamation is even a popular theme in Indian movies and television.

Even their names give away their dual identities. Most traditional Indian names get shortened or get Americanized. Alok becomes Al, Suburamanyam becomes Subu or even Sue etc. Mainstream Americans find it hard to pronounce some of the traditional tongue twisting Indian names and they are forced to anglicize their name for other's convenience. They prefer English names at school and many Coconuts have two names – one used only at home and the other used mostly outside.

What the Coconuts do for entertainment also gives valuable clues about their identity formation. The Coconut guys played football (the American way) and basketball. "My cousins in India keep talking of cricket scores. I can't make head or tail of that game. I know it is something like our baseball", said a Coconut. Indian-American youth played sports on a segregated basis, usually with or against other Indian or South Asian teams.

Young Indian women, as compared to their male peers, probably encounter more pressure in their attempt to negotiate between the boundaries of family life and selfhood. Though still expected by their parents to fulfill the role of obedient daughters, enter into matrimony and perform the cycle of domestic responsibilities, these women aspire to explore what the new world offers. Kiran who was born and raised in New Jersey in a predominantly Indian neighborhood, recalled that during her college days her attempts to shape her own selfhood were constantly thwarted by her working class parents, and she had to suppress her personal ambition to be an investment banker. Her parents wanted her to study enough to attract decent marriage proposals and get her married as soon as possible.

Indian movies are quite popular with the Coconut generation and Bollywood productions are normally rated above the Hollywood. The English sub-titles in Indian films have played a crucial role in making it more appealing to this generation. Indian film songs are also gaining in popularity, but Coconut generation has a wider range of taste when it comes to music. Being pulled simultaneously in different directions, young Indian American men and women are seeking an easy way out. Although both cultures are worlds apart, they learn to live in both as a coping mechanism – constantly traveling between the two worlds. Such extensive cultural travel causes this generation to suffer from "cultural jet-lags".

The citizenship is another conflicting matter for Indian-Americans. Passports have become symbolic of the larger reality and have determined one's identity and loyalty to a nation. Some of the Coconuts are American citizens by birth, while others are naturalized citizens. In either case they have very little national identification with India. The immigrant generation considers American citizenship very highly as they have to work hard to obtain it in order to sponsor the rest of their family to this country. They believe American citizenship can help the next generation to get a headstart when it comes to social or economic ascent. The recent bill in Indian parliament to give dual citizenship for people of Indian origin in America and many other developed nations will further complicate this identity development process. We may have to wait and see how the Coconut generation will respond to the dual citizenship provision.

The Coconut generation learns about America at school and about India at home. They learn about George Washington and Abraham Lincoln at school, while parents tell stories of Mahatma Gandhi and Jawaharlal Nehru. At school they learn about the American ideals of freedom and individualism while at home they are taught about *ahimsa* (non-violence) and *dharma* (duty).

An extraordinary measure of cultural blending is happening with the Coconut generation. It was best described by Arun,

> I like American breakfasts and Indian *thali* lunches. My tongue developed a fondness for curries and soup. I can survive hottest spices and bland food. I am adroit at eating with fork and spoon and with hands. I say grace in English and bedtime prayers in Hindi. I like both *kurta-pajama* and suit with tie. Best holidays I had was in Kulu-Manali and Hawaii. I put up a tree at Christmas and celebrate *Diwali* (the Indian festival of lights). I have gone to churches on Sundays and have visited many other religious places. I

am dating a Caucasian now, but hope to get married to an Indian girl someday. I speak to my parents and siblings in Hinglish (blend of Hindi and English). I listen mostly to Indi-pop and read Indian novels in English. I am all mixed up, you see.

They live not in 'either-or' world, but 'both-and' world. Until very recently such divergent lifestyles could never converge in one place. When paradoxes paralyzed one generation, the next generation thrived on it. The earlier era always tried to establish order and sequence, while the later era increases the disorder and flourishes on chaos. The Coconut generation is making the transition from the mechanistic modern world to a turbulent post-modern world.

Similarly Dr. Sengupta wants to have her identity both ways: "I am, I know, both Indian and American." She arrived here in the early 90s to pursue her doctoral research and was planning to return after five years. "I met my husband at school, who had come from another part of India and was in the same department, just ahead of me by a couple of years. After he finished, he got a good job and we bought a home close to the university. I feel very American in my thinking, yet celebrate many Indian ways. I will never be complete without both." Such ambivalence of living in two worlds causes Coconuts as well as some recent immigrants to absorb the repulsions and attractions or rejection and acceptance of both.

The term 'bi-cultural' was popularly used among many ethnic literature to describe those who not only speak two languages (like Hindi and English), but also can move between two cultures. Another term that has become popular to describe this blended nature of the younger generation is "third culture kids". Many seemingly bi-culturals are not bi-cultural any more, but have created a third culture that is neither Indian culture nor the culture of the host country. This is also true of children of inter-racial marriages, missionary kids and a trend among emerging generations everywhere.

Third culture kids are cross-culturally mobile children. Their emergent lifestyle produces a third culture that lacks national or cultural boundaries. Third-Culture kids are marginal, mobile in body, soul, and intellect. Their roots lie in uprootedness. They fit in everywhere and nowhere in particular. They are simultaneously insiders and outsiders. They develop a sense of belonging to all the cultures of which they've been a part of without having a sense of identity in any. No place is home for them, yet they are home everywhere. They are looking beyond geography or culture to define and own them. This is truly the generation that is the product and producer of globalization.

Culture: More Than *Sanskriti*[3]

What is the Coconut subculture? It is more elusive than I had ever thought it would be. What makes it so difficult to understand is that the Indian American generation subculture consists of a broad spectrum of subcultures within itself. And the spectrum is a dynamic too – constantly changing as Coconuts keep moving constantly along the spectrum. By the time you defined the subculture, it has morphed into another entity altogether. Thus, factors shaping the subculture becomes more important than the shape of it. Some of the factors are – ethnicity, acculturation rate, socio-cultural interactions, exposure to western culture, value system, home environment, community, faith, and educational level.

Vivek articulated the Coconut subculture succinctly. "We are more western than we would like to admit it and more Indian than we would like to admit it. We are neither Indian nor American. We are both Indian and American." We should be careful not to jump to conclusions about them by their looks (color and Indian features), or by their accent (American). There are shades of brownness and whiteness mixed together in them. That is why I prefer to call them Coconuts – brown on the outside and white on the inside. We must not pre-judge by mere externalities, but dig deeper. Indian cultural norms are inadequate for fully understanding their idiosyncrasies. Eating *tandoori or dosa,* not dating, achieving monetary success, and learning to cook are too superficial for determining their unique bend. Look deeper and try harder to understand them. The ministry to the second generation will depend on understanding this unique subculture and duality of personhood.

> An understanding of culture is basic to Christian youth work... youth ministry is not only shaped by youth culture, but also shaped by the culture of the church. This means that Christian youth workers must be culturally bilingual.
>
> **Pete Ward**

The community has a strong element of Indian culture. It is not just a collection of individuals gathered together for a common purpose. Every individual is expected to submit to familial and communal norms; upon deviation an elder could impose severe sanctions and in extreme cases, deviant members can be ostracized. The pressure to conform to family norms and expectation can and does cause acute strain in relationships.

They are constantly jumping back and forth between the two worlds. All expressions and meanings get re-interpreted afresh as they move between the cultural lines, if there is one. For them, boundary is all blurred, yet they are always aware where they are. Their personality and culture is divided between these two worlds. They quickly develop a translator mechanism, which is constantly deciphering both world inputs to each other and trying to make sense of it all. As long as the two worlds are somewhat compatible or some correlations can be made, the inner processing for the Coconut generation is manageable.

But when the two worlds crash head on, it creates enormous undercurrents for the Coconuts. The Americanization stresses on individuality, while the Indian culture values familial. Eastern thought reveres authority; Western thought challenges authority. When the tectonic plates collide deep within them, it sends giant tsunami waves to the shores of adolescent Coconuts, washing some of the things they were holding on to into the deep. When there is nothing to hang on to, many are swept away by the receding waves and drown.

The Indian-ness and American-ness are mixed up into one concoction. Without either, it will lack the effect. It is so perfectly mixed up that they cannot be separated. This in-between-ness is not an empty transitional zone but creative cultural expressions. This fusion of the East and West springs forth new creative energy. This "creative creolization" along borders gives rise to hybrid populations that are said to "subversively appropriate and creolize master codes, decentering, destabilizing, and carnivalizing dominant forms through `strategic inflections' and `re-accentuations.'"[4] People who combine the best of Eastern and Western modes of thinking will have an advantage over those who think exclusively West or East.

The bicultural people can switch the cultural frame within which they operate depending on cues from situations. The generational response varies from choosing one over the other in all circumstances to choose a response depending on the issue. They have become adept at dealing with multiple complexities with multiple responses without any coherent, universal, meaning giving system.

Brown Shell: Hard Nut to Crack

There is an undeniable Indian side of the Coconut generation. Some ignore it; others pretend it doesn't exist, while still others wear masks, but brownness cannot be rubbed away easily. I am not just talking about color of the skin, but ineffable Indian-ness that is intrinsic to Indian Diaspora worldwide. Some Indians are fairer, some darker, but we all still exhibit the same collective tendencies. How we think and feel, our worldview, orientation, inclinations, attachments, etc. have innate common features.

The brown-ness of the Coconut generation is hard to penetrate through. Do not be fooled to group them with the immigrant generation because of the color of their skin, facial features, or other ethnic peculiarities. We must get past the brown side of things to get to the heart of the matter. If you have seen a Coconut, you know what I mean when I say the brown-ness of the Coconut generation is a hard nut to crack. Both Indian community churches and American churches grapple with their varying shades of brown-ness of the Coconut generation.

Ashok, a leader of a college fellowship in New Jersey readily agreed Indian influence in his life. "I definitely feel more American, but my family instilled a lot of values and traditions and Indian culture into me, and I try to retain as much of it as possible," he said. Even as they seems to embrace free spirited American culture readily, they know the strength of the Indian culture deep down inside and do not want to give it up either.

The dilemma of the brown shell is more complicated than we tend to think. A few years ago, I was debriefing Mike and Sunil on their first short-term mission trip to India. Mike described his trip, "I was visiting my home country, my people, people who looked like me, right? But when I landed in Mumbai airport in the middle of the night, a crowd pounced on me asking for dollars.

Some tried to offer a taxi ride to the hotel, while some others tried to sell me fake Nike shoes. How did they know I am not a native? Why did they not see me as their own? I was dressed like most teenagers and spoke whatever little Hindi I knew, trying to hide my Americanness, but it was futile. I am seen as a foreigner in my own ethnic home country! The trip has shown me how American I have become and more than I thought I was."

Go beyond the shell. Get past the hardness of the exterior and discover the tender side of their inner life. The Coconut generation is much deeper and more complex than mere skin color. Sometime a hard knock alone can crack open the hard shell. If you have seen how Coconuts are broken, you know what I mean. Their unique experience of being the emerging generation in a multicultural postmodern world has toughened their exteriors, but like all teenagers they have a softer inner core that is looking for meaningful relationships in order to discover themselves and their mission in this world.

White Flesh: Born in the USA

The Coconut generation displays an innate white-ness in their inner self. If we can get beyond their brown-ness, you will be surprised to see how 'white' they have become. I use white mostly as the color of the host majority culture. In some cases, the inner side is painted black for Indian second generation who have assimilated with African or African-American culture.

One of the clear distinctions of the Coconut generation is that they are natural citizens of America. Their parents came on employment or student visas and many become permanent residents or naturalized citizens subsequently. But second generations are born citizens. They are natives in the "foreign" land. They had no "Ellis Island" experience, Americanism comes naturally to them. From the day they step into daycare or the first day at school, they are constantly imbibing from everything around them.

It is strange for anyone to feel like a foreigner in one's own country. When you are treated as a foreigner by everyone, such feelings flood our consciousness. In spite of the fact that you were born in America, most others still consider you an immigrant. Vijay told me a story of a recent interview he had for a leading media company. Vijay has been born and raised in Boston and his parents were one of the early immigrants in America. Frustrated, he said, "They asked me, 'Where I am from?' and I answered, "I am an American, born and raised right here in Boston. They kept asking 'Where are you really from?'" He continued, "they wanted to me say that I am from India, but how can I? I have only visited India twice in my whole life and that too for a week each when I was in elementary school. I do not know anyone there. I will be lying, if I say I am from India. I know nothing about India. Why should they make such a fuss about it anyway? Or they should ask what my ethnic roots are? To which I do not mind admitting that my parents are from India. But I am not from India. Do you see the difference, Sam?"

The second generation, in their early teens, show a whiteness that is not firmed up yet. I call them Tender Coconuts. The inner flesh is in its formative stage and only when they are done with early college does some of the whiteness fully find its place. Nevertheless, you can see a whiteness and lots of sweet water in tender Coconuts. Depending on where people are in their journey of Americanization, there is a varying degree of absorption of American-ism through the inevitable process of cultural osmosis. There are two solutions that are competing to get to the heart of the Coconut generation. One is the higher concentration of American-ness at school, with friends and through the media, and the other is the Indian-ness at home, church and with Indian friends. As the Coconut generation grows up in the American society, a certain amount of American-ness is seeping through the Coconut shells, turning the flesh more white.

Coconut Subculture: Conform or Preserve

The brown side of Coconuts embraces family/community, structure, emotional restraint, respect for authority etc; while the white side of Coconut prefers individuality, autonomy, expressiveness and creativity. These are fundamentally opposed sets of values and the Coconut lives through this tension every day of his/her life. The rate of assimilation to either of these cultures (mostly western culture) will determine his/her worldview.

Before going to college, most Coconuts see themselves as 'an average American teenager' who wants to assimilate to be like other Anglos. Assimilation simply means speaking only English, dressing like their American peers, going on dates, associating primarily with white people and even distancing themselves from their parents' culture. A Temple University student in Philadelphia once told me, "When I was in high school, I did a lot of things that were anti-Indian. I didn't hang around with Indians. I did not want to be seen with my parents. I would avoid the Indian church and the community at all costs. I wasn't very proud to be an Indian. I even colored my hair, completely avoided Indian clothes and food."

A couple of years ago, another young man confided to me, "I am not sure what I want to do in life. But I am very certain what I do not want to do. More precisely who I do not want be like." I thought maybe he would discover his vocational choices more by a process of elimination and asked him about what options he had ruled out. He replied, "I am very clear about this. I do not want to be like my parents! They work all the time. Making money is their sole passion in life. There should be more to life than mere material things. More material things will not quench my thirst." That was a shocking revelation! A clear pointer to the reality of deeper longings of this generation, who are looking beyond the material to the spiritual. True, like many migrant communities the first generation worked very hard to realize their American dream, sometimes even at the expense of their children. Thinking they are doing all things for their children, yet unaware of their deeper heart longings. Consequently, children have seen first hand the fallacy of making a living and not having a life.

East vs West: Differing Notions of Culture

A fundamental difference between Eastern and Western worldviews is with respect to an understanding of guilt and shame cultures. Just as the Western world is more guilt and performance oriented, the Eastern world is more shame and being oriented. In the East, the public perception and communal thinking is far more valued than one's own conviction or individuality. Anthropology informs us that cultures may be classified by their emphasis on using either shame or guilt to socially regulate the activities of their members. The social consequence of 'getting caught' is seen as more important than the individual's feeling or the experience; defilement or contamination is a bigger issue than depravity itself. Most Asian cultures, for example Chinese, Japanese, and Indian are considered shame-based cultures, while European and modern American cultures are considered guilt-based cultures.

Guilt tells me I *made* a mistake. Shame tells me that I *am* a mistake. If my behavior is wrong, I can correct it and change. If my very being is flawed, I am without hope for change. Dr. Paul Hiebert, an American anthropologist who spent many years of mission work and research in India had analyzed the guilt and shame based cultures in detail. According to him,

> Guilt is a feeling that arises when we violate the absolute standards of morality within us, when we violate our conscience. A person may suffer from guilt although no one else knows of his or her misdeed; this feeling of guilt is relieved by confessing the misdeed and making restitution. True guilt cultures rely on an internalized conviction of sin as the enforcer of good behavior, not, as shame cultures do, on external sanctions. Guilt cultures emphasize punishment and forgiveness as ways of restoring the moral order; shame cultures stress self-denial and humility as ways of restoring the social order.[5]

On the contrary, a guilt based culture is communal just as guilt based culture is individualistic. About shame based cultures, Dr. Hiebert had this to say:

> Shame is a reaction to other people's criticism, an acute personal chagrin at our failure to live up to our obligations and the expectations other have of us. In true shame oriented cultures, every person has a place and a duty in the society. One maintains self-respect, not by choosing what is good rather than what is evil, but by choosing what is expected of one. Personal desires are sunk in the collective expectation. Those who fail will often turn their aggression against themselves instead of using violence against others. By punishing themselves they maintain their self-respect before others, for shame cannot be relieved as guilt can be, by confession and atonement. Shame is removed and honor restored only when a person does what society expects of him or her in the situation, including committing suicide if necessary.[6]

In the Coconut generation where both cultures converge, they experience both guilt *and* shame. As they simultaneously and repeatedly live between guilt and shame based cultures, their woes are multiplied. They seem to get a raw deal from both ends, even as they try to make the most of both cultures. In-betweenness is as much a blessing as it is a curse. An understanding of cultures in these underlying terms helps to gain insight into the uniqueness and struggle of the Coconut generation.

Assimilation: Taking It In

Assimilation is the process of ethnic boundary reduction as a result of interaction with other ethnic groups. Cultural assimilation involves adoption of the cultural traits of one's new host country like language, religion, clothing styles, diet, and other norms, values, and beliefs. There is a wide range of theories to explain immigrant experiences ranging from renunciation of the ancestral culture in favor of the host culture, blending of cultures, to upholding cultural distinctiveness. This continuum of understanding also emerged over time with increasing migration of various ethnic populations from around the world into the United States. The early twentieth century immigrant experience was commonly understood as Anglo-conformity theory[7] - a complete renunciation of the immigrants ancestral culture in favor of the behavior and values of the Anglo-Saxon majority group. Then, in the second half of twentieth century the 'melting pot' was the most common theory of merger between the majority culture and immigrant cultures. But presently not much "melting" is happening, rather immigrants are preserving their traditional culture resulting in a multicultural society.

Cultural assimilation or acculturation means taking on the ways of the host society in matters of dress, diet, lifestyle and worldview. Other examples of assimilation include structural, marital, identificational and civic. According to many migration studies, the most critical among them all, for minorities, is the structural assimilation. Once a group enters social, economic, and political institutions of the host society, it will lead to marital assimilation, breaking down the ethnic barriers and distinctive values of one's native land.

Depending on the time of migration and the rate of assimilation, different groups can exist at different stages of the assimilation process. Degrees of prejudice, discrimination, segregation, and racism determine the level of active participation in the mainstream American society. For early immigrants, acculturation was primarily functional – learning enough about the host culture in order to survive and retaining their home culture. They also isolated themselves from mainstream society to preserve their culture and to avoid dilution, not to mention the hostility of American culture to the early migrants through racism, inequality and absence of social, economic and political mobility.

Their racial origin – the visible characteristics of their bodies (color of skin, hair color, eye, facial features, religious symbols etc.) and social norms (family, rituals, religion etc.) set the immigrants apart from the larger society. They suffered social segregation, economic discrimination and legal handicaps because of their perceived physical and biological differences.

Acculturation works best for the second generation of the immigrants, because they have the opportunity to go through the American school system and are expected to participate in mainstream society. For the first generation, their sole pursuit was economic advancement and to provide opportunities for their children. Thus, they are mentally distant from the dominant culture and hope to return to their home country.

Assimilation Matrix: Where Do I Fit?

In the last chapter of *Asian Americans: Emerging Minorities*, Harry Kitano and Roger Daniels present a model for classifying Asian Americans into four categories based on two variables – Assimilation and Ethnic Identity. I have adapted the model to the specifics of Indians in America and arrived at 4 subgroups among Coconut generation as in figure 4.1. When we draw the varying degrees of ethnic identity on the X-axis and varying degrees of assimilation on the Y-axis, it produces four quadrants. The assimilation variable (American-ness) "includes integration into the schools, the workplace, social groupings, as well as identification with the majority and marital assimilation. The ethnic identity (Indian-ness) dimension is essentially a pluralistic adaptation, focusing on the retention of ethnic ways."[8] The parameters could include food habits, dress code, language skills, association with social groups, attitudes, friends, nationality etc. It could be divided into broad categories as physical, legal, vocational, psychological, cultural, ideological (religious, political), etc.

Figure 4.1 Types of Coconuts

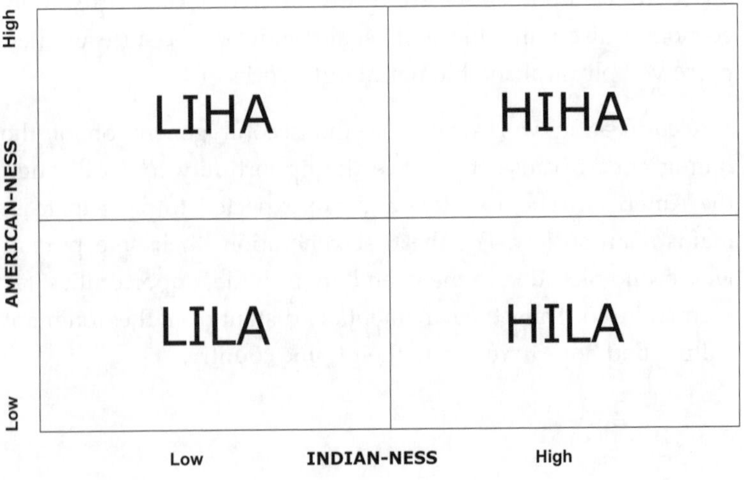

High	LIHA	HIHA
AMERICAN-NESS		
Low	LILA	HILA
	Low **INDIAN-NESS** High	

Low Indian-ness, Low American-ness (LILA)

This group of Indian Americans show very limited assimilation and are unsure of their ethnic identity also. They are a disenchanted and disillusioned lot. They have failed to find their place in both cultures, and it is indicative of their prevailing identity confusion. They are critical of both Indian and American ways and have not gained any appreciation for either culture and could be considered acutely marginalized.

LILAs have a deflated sense of ethnic identification. They feel ashamed of their looks, skin color or other ethnic features. If you dig deeper, you may come across experiences of racism or other bitter past experiences from within the community. You can see signs of loneliness, depression and lack of direction. They isolate themselves from mainstream American ways and also from Indian communities.

To develop a healthy sense of identity, LILAs must find people and resources that can help them to safely explore the majority culture and the Indian culture. They must handle their fears and past experiences with the help of caring relationships and in light of the truths of the gospel of Jesus Christ. They must begin to interact with others and avoid seclusion. Ask God to help you grow in appreciation of your uniqueness and journey of discovering your self and his purposes for you.

High Indian-ness, Low American-ness (HILA)

This person is more Indian than American. They tend to preserve the values of the world they left behind. The recent immigrants (FOB) and the Coconuts that have grown up in exclusive Indian American communities tend to fall into this group. Some HILAs even consider Indian culture superior to all other cultures (ethnocentricism) and always finds fault with everything American. They associate more with others who have a high sense of ethnic identity. They spend most of the time within their ethnic settings and maintain close ties with folks back in India, often called "ghetto" mentality. They are otherwise called Traditionalists.

HILAs mostly speak in Indian languages and often maintain an Indian accent when speaking English. They are constantly trying to re-create the Indian way of life and will not refer to themselves as American. They hold critical views or distrust of the dominant culture and institutions. They show pride in their Indian heritage and relish traditional cuisines, dress and the like. They worship in Indian community churches or temples and have no exposure to American churches. Dating or marrying non-Indians is very unlikely for HILAs and they are open to seeking alliances from relatives. Most of them agree to arranged marriages and marrying girls or boys from India.

HILAs need to recognize that the ability to relate to dominant culture is an essential part of advancing socially and economically in the United States. Learning about American ways does not necessarily erode one's ethnic identification. They must overcome their racist prejudices and heal from the distorted ethnocentric conceptions. They must seek divine help in developing a healthy understanding of values, beliefs, traditions and worldviews of others. Cross-cultural exposure, friendships, resources etc. can be very helpful in developing such mindset.

Low Indian-ness, High American-ness (LIHA)

This person is more American than Indian. It is not uncommon for many members of this group to be completely cut off from India and Indian American communities. LIHAs are very comfortable interacting with Americans and are open to dating/marrying non-Indians. They bear a very thin layer of browness that is not very hard either. In fact, they do not want to be associated with brown folks and might carry some negative feelings or stereotypes against Indian-ness. They are generally called the Assimiliationists.

LIHAs are able to integrate into the majority culture with ease and have many American friends. They may speak or understand very little of Indian languages and spend very little time within their ethnic community. They may have grown up in places with very few Indians or intentionally isolated themselves from ethnic communities. They are comfortable being a part of white student groups or organizations and American churches. Their parents have not exposed them to Indian culture and have no contact whatsoever with cousins/relatives back in India.

LIHAs need to explore and embrace their ethnic self. Interact with their parents and find out more about their ancestry and immigration journey. If possible, they should visit India and get to know their extended families. In addition, they should interact with Indian-American communities in the United States. They need to grow to acknowledge their ethnicity as a divine gift and celebrate it.

High Indian-ness, High American-ness (HIHA)

This person is able to integrate well into the majority culture and still retain ethnic distinctiveness. They are able to speak English, one or more Indian language or are in the process of acquiring Indian language skills. They are at home in white neighborhoods and Indian communities; effortlessly traveling back and forth. They love many things from both Indian and western cultures

– food, clothing, music, dance, movies, etc. It is hard for HIHAs to choose one culture over the other, and they tend to make the best of both worlds. They are otherwise called Biculturals.

HIHAs serve as a bridge to their immigrant parents/community and the American culture. They show a strong sense of self and relate to either cultural contexts in a healthy manner. They might date and marry people from either race and are less likely to marry people directly from India. They are able to objectively see the good and bad of both cultures and are inclined to make informed choices. They visit relatives back in India and have traveled to other places to explore their ethnic roots. HIHAs exhibit high tolerance for contradictions and operate in a culturally pluralistic fashion.

No matter what you do, HIHAs are often misunderstood by one group or the other. They need to show higher levels of maturity and patience in coping with both worlds. The borderland existence is hard and takes a toll if they do not find other compatible people.

In most youth groups where I have done this study, LILAs and HIHAs are a smaller lot, which is understandable due to the strong kinship culture and socialization trends in Indian churches. Most are LIHAs or HILAs. The LILAs are a confused bunch and their sense of insecurity is devastating to their development, especially in matters of faith. The coming generations will show greater assimilation trends and if they continue to discover their ethnicity, we will have more HIHAs or we will be left with LIHAs. This grouping greatly depends on life stages. In their early teens, most Coconuts tend to fall into HILA and in high school and college years they resemble LIHAs. In their mid-teens some become LILAs, mostly out of their disillusionment with their complex self. The family of origin and home environment plays a central role in determining which group they are inclined towards.

Being in the formative stages of identity development, young people constantly move between the quadrants. Their place is not permanent at all. In fact, some experience all four quadrants in the same day. This grid is only intended at closely analyzing the varying degree of assimilation patterns and ethnic identity discovery. We must boldly embrace all facets of our existence and find its purpose in God who created us within a specific ethnic setting and placed us in the American context. Instead of ignoring or denying any part of us, we must move towards experiencing wholeness and celebrate our uniqueness. It is only with such a healthy perspective that we can make a lasting difference with our lives and bring glory to the name of our God.

Hybrid Cultures: Blended Reality

People who grow Rose flowers are all too familiar with Hybridization. The process of cross-pollination and grafting techniques successfully produces roses of new colors, size, smell and shape. Hybrid cars are making inroads in America these days. Hybrids (bilinguals and biculturals) have an advantage in the corporate world. The computer world has many hybrids which are key to maintaining compatibility with emerging technologies and standards.

The unprecedented intermingling of cultures all over the world has led to the creation of new hybrid cultures. There was a time when people preserved cultural purity; but lately blended cultures are considered 'cool'.

At the very core hybrids show a duality of personality - two natures, two tendencies, and two personas woven together into one. Some see it as a divided self or as cultural schizophrenia, while others see it as double consciousness. "The idea of interconnectedness in-between leads us to a positive and self affirming understanding of marginality "in-both" worlds. This new self affirming definition complements the earlier self negating definition or the classical definition of the dominant group."[9]

Traditionally, mixed race people were marginalized and despised; cultural pedigree were cherished, but recent scholars see this status as uniquely privileged; possessing an ability to see at once inside and out. The in between-ness has become a place of power and influence. The idea of borderland is an attempt to wrestle with identities that do not fit neatly into master discourses of ethnicity, race and nation. The subaltern identity is the new identity existing between two competing identities. The margins have become the new center!

Latin American thinkers have helped us understand this with the concept of *mestizaje*, meaning "mixed-ness" or the status of being *mestizo*, or mixed blood. *Mestizaje* allows a society to draw equally on its diverse cultural inheritances. "The *mestizo* affirms both the identities received while offering something new to both."[10] *Mestizos* are uniquely qualified to question the arrogant claims to purity made by given races and states. Since they have no abiding city on earth, *mestizo* loyalty belongs neither to race nor nation, but the 'New Jerusalem' – the city of God.

In contemporary theology, *mestizaje* is so critical because it transcends traditional racial hierarchies. It thus comes closer to the New Testament goal of a society without racial privileges or domination, in which there is neither Jew nor Greek, Latino nor Anglo.[11] This is a potent theology for a world of de-racinated migrants and wanderers in a globalized world, who define their identities in terms of not roots, but more by routes.

Virgilo Elizondo presents Jesus as a *mestizo* son of Galilee's mixed and marginalized society, who enters the great city of Jerusalem in order to challenge its wealth, to confront the racial arrogance of the culturally pure elites.[12]

To Ponder About:

1. List ten characteristics that will define Indian-ness and American-ness for you. To each of the parameters rate yourself on a scale of 1 to 10 and sum total of your rating is the Indian-ness quotient and American-ness quotient. On a scale of 0 – 100 in the Assimilation Matrix of figure 4.1, where would you place yourself. E.g (40, 38) is LILA; (55, 40) is HILA; (45, 70) is LIHA; (75, 80) is HIHA.

2. To which quadrant are you moving towards? What is helping or hindering you to move there.

3. What areas of culture do you feel the pull to be strongest and weakest? Why?

4. What are the advantages and disadvantages of the hybrid cultural identities?

5. What helped you most in growing in ethnic identity? What resources are there in your community? How could you help someone else in their ethnic identity discovery?

Endnotes

[1] Rudyard Kipling,The Ballard of East and West, 1889.

[2] Raymond Scupin, Ethnicity in *Race and Ethnicity,* (Englewood Cliff, NJ: Prentice Hall, 2003) 69.

[3] Hindi word for Culture.

[4] Smadar Lavie and Ted Swedenburg. "Introduction," in *Displacement, Diaspora, and Geographies of Identity.* Eds. Smadar Lavie and Ted Swedenburg, (Durham: Duke University Press, 1996) 1-25.

[5] Paul G. Hiebert, *Anthropological Insights for Missionaries*, (Grand Rapids: Baker Book House, 1985) 213.

[6] Ibid. 212.

[7] Milton Gordon, *Assimilation in American Life: The Role of Race, Religion, and National Origins*, (New York: Oxford University Press, 1964) 85.

[8] Harry Kitano and Roger Daniel, *Asian Americans: Emerging Minorities,* (Englewood Cliff, NJ: Prentice Hall, 1988) 191.

[9] Jung Lee, *Marginality: The Key to Multicultural Theology*, (Minneapolis: Fortress Press, 1995) 47.

[10] Virgilio P. Elizondo, *The Future is Mestizo,* ed. (Boulder: University Press of Colorado, 2000) 84.

[11] Philip Jenkins, *The Next Christendom: The Coming of Global Christianity,* (New York: Oxford University Press, 2002) 116.

[12] Virgilo P. Elizondo, *Galilean Journey: The Mexican American Promise* (Maryknoll, New York: Orbis, 1983).

5

Longing for Belonging:
Family and Community of Coconuts

"...I am the marginal man between two forces,
and possibly I will be crushed.
But that is where God has placed me,
and I have accepted the vocation."
– Desmond Tutu

Jhumpa Lahiri, a Pulitzer Prize winning Asian Indian second generation author shared her dilemma of where she belongs. "I never know how to answer the question "Where are you from?" If I say I'm from Rhode Island, people are seldom satisfied. They want to know more, based on things such as my name, my appearance, etc. Alternatively, if I say I'm from India, a place where I was not born and have never lived, this is also inaccurate. It bothers me less now. But it bothered me growing up, the feeling that there was no single place to which I fully belonged."[1]

Where is home? A simple question once upon a time, but these days bring ever more complex answers. Home is becoming more intangible and incoherent. In the contemporary world, where everything is global and fragmented, home has become more difficult to describe than it was for our forefathers. What once might have resembled a well-creased snapshot now looks more like an MTV video - ever changing, split second moving images with varied camera angles. The Coconut generation is on a journey toward home. They are on a discovery trail to find where they really belong. The longing to belong and the sense of security it can provide is fundamental to all, but is more pronounced in hybrid generations. They live in a creative tension generated by fragmented visions of "home" and "abroad." Assimilation comes often at the high cost of alienation from hearth and home.

Parivar[2]: Born Into or Choose?

None of us chose to be born into the families that we belong to. If given a choice, perhaps some would choose otherwise. There may be exceptions, though. Family still remains among the top two influencers in adolescence, while the other is peers. Coming from a closely-knit, family-oriented Indian culture, family has made an even more decisive influence on the Coconut generation than other ethnic emerging generations. Without stereotyping, however wild or individualistic the Coconuts appear, they are much more aware of their family and its importance in their lives than their American counterparts.

Not only do we inherit the color of our skin and ethnicity, but sense of self and belonging also come from our family. In some cases, the family of origin might stand in the way of discovering our true longing and belonging. Some are affirmed and aided in their search for home, and for others it is a stumbling block. Many Coconuts grow up in dysfunctional homes and their constant attempt is to distance themselves from it in order to avoid any further damage. In other cases, the family isolates Coconuts from the "contamination" of the real world. My friend Srinivasan was more forthright about his sheltered life, "I lived in a completely insulated Tamil world until I became an adult. When we moved to Houston, I was eighteen months old. My mother wore traditional dress and cooked *sambar, rasam and dosas* almost everyday;

we never cooked or went out to eat Western food. We spoke Tamil and we even had a *puja* room in every home we have lived. My parents had a circle of Tamilian friends; they didn't mix with the locals or even with other Indians. I was constantly told that Tamil 'ways' are better than American ways. My family was the only world I knew for many years."

> **Every Christian family ought to be, as if it were, a little church.**
> **Jonathan Edwards**

In India, family roles were clearly defined and were more traditional in nature, men being breadwinners and women were homemakers. Men also held enormous authority and power in all matters concerning home and outside the home. The household chores were done mostly by women, even if they were employed outside of the home. The children were expected to be obedient and compliant. But having grown up in a more egalitarian and functional society like America, the second generation tends to question authority and expect logical reasoning for parental actions.

Extended families are important to all Indians. Although they live as nuclear families in America, they keep close ties with their relatives. Many early immigrants brought their siblings and lived close by for support, creating their own clans.

But when one's blood relations are far away and very little contact exists on a regular basis, they tend to create surrogate families of their own. All adult males are considered 'uncles' and all adult females are addressed 'aunties', even when there is no blood relationship. The members to this new extended family are chosen, mostly from similar educational and socio-cultural backgrounds and who will support their generational aspirations. Rather than settle down into traditional roles, the Coconut generation has formed an Urban Tribe – "an intricate community of young people who live and work together in various combinations, form regular rituals, and provide the support of an extended family." They are re-defining what family, friendship and relational commitment is all about, sending shock waves to the immigrant generation in the process. They are living happily in groups of their own choosing and making. Whether married or single, married/dating outside the race or inside, as successful as their parents or not, they are basically changing all the rules. They are guided by strong bonds of kinship among them and are willing to forsake all else for its sake. They value the Indian concept of extended families and are doing it in the "American" way – making the best of both worlds.

Many of the first generation immigrants display ethnocentrism - a preference for one's own kind and their way over others'. Without an adequate support system, the early immigrants have suffered much more discrimination than their children or later immigrants and they tend to think stereotypically. It might also lead them to cut themselves and their children off from the larger world around them. Thus, some Coconuts remained largely cocooned from the real world. Their families erected impenetrable walls that isolated them from wider reality. Asha confessed her cultural aloneness, "I discovered other Indians when I went away to college from a friend. She introduced me to this overseas Indian culture; things like Hindi language, Bollywood movies, *Gujurati tali* etc. Some things were shocking like not all Indians are Christians; in fact most of them are Hindus. I even have a boyfriend from Delhi. Of course, I do not tell my parents anything."

Out-marriages (marrying outside the Indian community) are growing among the second generation. One's ethnicity, caste or religion does not play as much a pivotal role in match making as it did for his/her parents. The inter-racial marriage, mostly among women (also true of other Asians), is a result of the Coconut generation desiring not to marry men who expected them to behave in traditional female roles. This is often fueled by negative conditioning at home or in the neighborhood they grew up in where women were poorly treated by their husbands. They expected more egalitarian roles and had to look outside the Indian community for life partners.

Popular movies bring out many satirical similarities with Indian culture and inter-generational dynamics within families. *My Big Fat Greek Wedding* is one such movie. It portrayed family ties as something both to escape from and to embrace. They can never be accepted fully, or rejected completely. The Coconut generation is walking the tightrope, balancing between the past and forging ahead into the future. Another popular film that demonstrates the tension between the immigrant generation and their children's aspiration is *Bend it like Beckham,* by Gurinder Chadha, depicting the British Indian girlhood. It beautifully portrays the conflicting expectations between the generations and how differently they handle the issues.

Many immigrant churches have followed the American model of youth ministry in their own churches by isolating youths from the adult world, particularly parents. The notion that parents do not "know" anything about

> **After that whole generation had been gathered to their fathers, another generation grew up, who knew neither the Lord nor what he had done for Israel.**
> **Judges 2:10 (NIV)**

youth issues and "when-I-was-your-age" talks make kids run the other direction. In addition, the second generation made it difficult for their parents to be involved in any meaningful ways other than the "give me car keys, some money and leave us alone" mentality.

In the mid 90s, Mark DeVries cried out that there is crisis in traditional youth ministry in American churches and suggested greater involvement of family, both immediate and church, in the ministry to the youths. He presented a new rationale for a paradigm shift in our approach to working with teenagers. The age-appropriate, compartmentalized approach to ministry of churches was becoming ineffective, which called greater involvement from youths' respective families and the church family. This was no surprise for the Asian Indian community, who has always valued their kinship oriented culture over the extreme individualistic style they have seen here in the West.

Youth ministry is not about ministering to the youth alone anyway. It is about getting everyone involved - parents, siblings, friends, teachers and everything else that affects the youth, in ministering to the youths. Getting them to play their respective roles in accordance with the grand master plan of ministering to the emerging generation is the real challenge. According to Search Institute research, "Positive development [in young people] requires constant exposure to interlocking system of support, control and structure. In the ideal, young people – via family, school, community organizations and religious institutions – constantly interact with caring, principled adults."[3] These adult interactions with them should move the youth to a real encounter with the living God; a growing awareness of God's purpose for their lives and owning the faith for themselves, rather than a "hand-me-down" faith of their forefathers.

Generation Gap: Bridging the Gulf

After I preached at the Sunday morning service, the parent of a youth that I had been working with for some time invited me to his home for lunch. I had a good time getting to know the family and updating them about youth ministry in the church. Later in the afternoon, the father began to complain, "My son isn't being fed", "Your youth service is focused on experience and doesn't have enough meat", "The group just doesn't know basic Christian doctrines", "it is only social" etc.

This wasn't the first time I heard that. I knew that there was no point in defending the youth programs at the church and felt convicted about a greater need to educate the parents and to equip them to minister to their kids effectively as well. I remembered when I had taken responsibility of the youth ministry at that church, a common view that adults held was - "we don't know what is going on with the youth. They gather together in the church basement every Sunday behind

> **"Even when I am old and gray, do not forsake me, O God, till I declare your power to the next generation, your might to all who are to come."**
> **Psalm 71:18 (NIV)**

closed doors …. We can hear some guitar strumming and singing… it is like a cult group, you know!"

I almost shot back, "Do you have any idea what your kids are going through otherwise?" But I held my reaction. I knew there was a lot of mistrust between parents and youth in immigrant churches. It was more than the typical parent vs. youth angst. It was a clash of generations, cultures and worldviews. The parents come from a traditional Indian culture and a modernistic perspective (if not pre-modern or traditional), while their kids were coming from an American post-modern perspective. What we are experiencing is not simply a generation gap but a fundamental shift in how people view the world. When clash happens across multiple lines, the challenge of youth ministry is acute.

The generation gap is a common problem in most ethnic churches. Believe it or not, youth leaders even 50 years ago also struggled with this issue; our children will find themselves different from us! When one generation becomes more pre-occupied with themselves and forgets to prepare the next generation for its calling, the health and strength of our church and community is at stake. When fathers and sons do not bond, mothers and daughters do not communicate, heritage is not transferred, and family bonds weaken - these are sure signs of the growing dysfunctionality of Indian homes. Each generation finds itself in worse shape than the generation that went before it.

Yet today, the gap has become a chasm with the change in prevailing worldviews from modernity to postmodernity. About the time that the church got really good at ministering in rational and linear terms, we peeked outside the front doors and found that the playing field had changed. Consider this—a primary value of modernity is knowing and communicating the right information. So, providing classes to youth on learning and communicating content are key aspects of ministry. However, a primary value of post-modernity is belonging and involvement. Therefore, allowing youth to experience authentic community and opportunities to serve together through ministry teams is essential. Both worldviews promote needed aspects of Christian growth, but they approach them from different angles.

Peter Drucker, a well-known management guru wrote in his book *Post-Capitalist Society*: "Every few hundred years in Western history there occurs a sharp transformation. Within a few short decades, society rearranges itself – its worldview, its basic values; its social and political structures; its art; its key institutions. Fifty years later, there is a new world. And the people born then cannot even imagine the world in which their grandparents lived and into which their parents were born. We are currently living through just such a transition."[4] The transitional generations bear the brunt of cataclysmic changes and their impact on the society.

In light of the obvious and growing generational rift, I have suggested intergenerational activities for many youth ministries. I have tried it myself a few times, but not without its drawbacks. The interaction between the generations can become a conduit for kids to hear first hand experience and the passion of those who are mature in their faith and building trust between them. But when the relationship is minimal or when parents do not exhibit vibrant faith, such forums can result in more damage than benefit you had intended. It ends up being a communal session to assert family obligations, expectations, and lists of do's don'ts; what parents went through to get here; comparisons, put-downs, guilt-producing, self-centered talks. Overall, intergenerational activities have positive impacts on both groups in getting to know each other a little better, provided that we do our homework properly.

What both generations need to recognize is that Christian faith comes in many flavors. It has taken root in all cultures of the world. Every culture and generation will incorporate their own uniqueness to their expression of faith. But what is important is to preserve the core beliefs and allow variations in its expressions. What will it take for the first generation to look beyond their own cultural Christianity and accept the

> **Community is the place where the person you least want to live with always lives.**
> **Henri Nouwen**

distinctive gifts and talents that will enrich the faith experiences of the generations to come? I hope the Coconut generation is willing to learn from their own struggle with parents, when their children want to make changes to their expressions, in the future.

Samuday[5]: Cultural or Biblical

E Pluribus Unum remains the national motto of the United States, but there no longer seems to be a consensus about what that should mean. The earlier assumption was that all different people and cultures would melt into a new homogenous entity (melting pot theory). But lately, the immigrant population has been preserving their uniqueness and is having more frequent interactions with folks back in home countries, thereby retaining much of their distinctions. So, at the present 'heat conditions', the contents of the American pot have become unmeltable! Or what happens when the melting pot itself melts? The contents end up in the fire! But our quest for community, whether among our own or not, remains a powerful force particularly among immigrants.

Table 5.1 Some Generational Differences

Immigrant Generation	Coconut Generation
Identity is ascribed; familial and caste related identity is imposed	Identity is achieved; familial and caste related identity is rejected
More communally minded	More individually minded
Individuals are viewed in terms of social hierarchy. Interpersonal relationship are formal with elaborate sense of rules	All persons are viewed equal. Interpersonal relationships are informal, flat without any complexities.
Social behaviors caste and religion related	Social behavior class related
Roles are well defined, gender based	Roles are flexible and loosely defined
Religion plays a dominant role in everyday life	Less religious, yet more spiritual
Religious rituals play a crucial role in daily life	Rituals are mostly secular; religious rituals are less important
Tend to be fatalistic and superstitious	Tend to be rational, logical and needing explanation
Emotions are kept in check	Feelings and emotions are expressed freely
Flexible attitude to time	Rigid attitude to time

Immigrant Generation	Coconut Generation
Goal and status driven	Relationship driven
Values uniformity	Values diversity
Leadership based on position and role	Leadership based on trust and relationship
Decision making is directive, mostly made by those who hold power in the group and rest is expected to follow through it	Decision making is participatory. Involvement of everyone is appreciated. Democratic in nature. All inputs are considered for its worth
Use internet for information	Use internet for relationship
Communications with others are often indirect and contextual, formal and planned	Communication with others is usually direct and to the point, informal and spontaneous
Emphasis on extended families	Prefers nuclear families, privacy and independence
Emphasis on collective responsibility and collective achievement	Emphasis on personal responsibility and individual achievement

The longing to attach or connect is one of the deepest longings of the human soul. To extend the idea of French mathematician and philosopher Blaise Pascal, we all have a "God-shaped" and "people-shaped" vacuum in our soul. We are internally wired for community and it is as fundamental to the soul as food, water and air are to our physical bodies. "To experience community is to know the joy of belonging, the delight at being known and loved, the opportunity for giving and growing, the safety of finding a true home.""[6] Mother Teresa left Albania to find her home in the streets of Calcutta. Henri Nouwen left teaching Harvard and Yale to find his home in the community of those with mental handicaps. Rich Mullins taught music to the children in the Native American reservations.

This does not mean that we need to leave everything and go somewhere else to find community. However, we do need to discover our greater purpose in life and align our passions to opportunities before us in order to make a lasting difference with our life along with other people who are equally passionate about it. When we find others who care about the

> **Aloneness can lead to loneliness.**
> **God's preventative for loneliness is intimacy - meaningful, open, sharing relationships with one another.**
> **In Christ we have the capacity for the fulfilling sense of belonging which comes from intimate fellowship with God and with other believers.**
> **Neil T. Anderson**

things that we care about and are committed to make this adventure together, we will feel at home. We are meant to find a community to share life's journey and God-given dreams together. We are not meant to do it alone.

The community was once confined by geographical area – as people who lived in a neighborhood. But technology and new rationale has re-defined community altogether. Community means a point of commonality, not of residence. Meaningful community boils down to one key matter: meaningful relationships; relationship that are authentic and enriching even as we bare our souls to others and help them discover their passions and purposes in life.

Here is what a young lady told me recently about her participation in other churches. She had grown up in a traditional Indian denominational church in Chicago and came to the saving knowledge of Christ at a campus fellowship. Upon graduation she came back to Chicago and began to attend the Axis service of the Willow Creek Community Church (a seeker-sensitive, multiethnic, contemporary, non-denominational mega-church in the western suburb of Chicago; the service is specially geared toward twenty-something age group with relevant music, visuals, skits and messages.) She enjoyed the music and teaching at Axis and even committed to be part of a small group fellowship and study. Recently one of the lead pastors of Axis met with her and a few of her Indian friends who go with her to Axis service regularly. The pastor asked, "What would it take to make Axis your home church?" I do not know what she said to the pastor. But this is what she told me, "I do not think I was offended by the question. But you know Axis will never be my home church. I go there for worship and good teaching. I get to hear good speakers who can talk on relevant issues and keep my attention. I enjoy the company of seekers and fellowship of other Indians who come there. But that will never be home for me. I go to the Indian church to serve and help my younger brother and sisters. I might not get much from it; yet that is home for me."

At the same time, I know of many in this generation who have cut the umbilical cords from the churches they had grown up in and have ventured into American churches, mostly in multiethnic bible or independent evangelical or 'new generation' churches. "I appreciate the ministry of my parent's church; I came to know the Lord there and served young people for a number of years. But that still remains my parent's church; I could never make it as my own. As one grows up, you need to move on and find your own faith community. And there are wonderful churches out there, if only we dare to look outside the box of immigrant church." Coconuts do not believe in the idea of inheriting denominational affiliation, but instead they "shop" around until they find a church that meets their needs, a place where they belong and where they feel comfortable in raising another generation.

Parampra: **Preserve or Evolve?**

One of the important aspects of all Diasporic communities, particularly in faith-matters, is traditions - the rituals and practices that transcend time and generations, giving them a connection to the past. It provides continuity and a notion of being a part of something greater from time immemorial. Many traditions are sources of strength for navigating through uncharted waters of life in America and the only sure thing that will stay with them for the future. In a unpredictable and fluid world, it brings stability and anchors our lives. For uprooted migrants, these practices provide a strong sense of rootedness, from where they can draw nourishment for meaning in the daily grind.

If something has worked for our forefathers and sustained them through ages, it is surely good for us and must come to our aid as well. Things that are tested and proven by many in the past are expected to produce similar results. In spiritual matters, traditions are more crucial and strictly enforced. Absence of traditions give rise to the risk of the dilution of values and any common standards of lifestyle in the community. The possible intrusion of heretical teachings is real.

However, tradition tends to set boundaries on life and discourages 'outside-the-box' thinking. The guardians of traditions are zealous in enforcing them and unwilling to entertain any reasoning behind the traditions. Most are unaware of its origin and how or why they came into being. How relevant they are for our times is often a non-negotiable matter.

> **Tradition is the living faith of those who are dead now. Traditionalism is the dead faith of those who are living now.**
> **- Historian Jaroslav Pelikan**

The popular musical and movie about the Jewish experience

in a foreign land and inter-generational conflict is the classic *Fiddler on the Roof*, which dramatizes the double mindedness about tradition. On the one hand we are drawn to tradition because it carries meaning, belonging, and it acts as glue that makes people stick together. On the other hand, it holds people back and represents the shackles of the past. Similar traditions of matchmaking, food, superstitions, religion, etc. can be easily seen among Indian Diaspora. Death of the tradition is portrayed as positive, inevitable and result of evolutionary process. The daughters stretched the age-old conceptions of the family and ended up marrying outside the community. One daughter gets around the matchmaker and marries for love – a tailor from the same village. The next daughter married a revolutionary leader from the city. The third daughter falls in love with a Gentile. This is too much for the poor father - the impulsive, old-fashioned patriarch, who finally gives in and life moves on. It is a story of assimilation ideology and celebration of death of tradition by younger generations. Likewise the Disney production, *Mulan* draws strength and guidance from her ancestral faith to challenge oppressive traditions.

Redeeming Traditions: New Meaning for Old

Traditions are not all bad. The way we have gone about enforcing them, may be. The churched Coconuts have developed such aversion toward traditions that mere mention of the word makes them repulsive, whether they understand its significance or not.

Our family and community may be celebrating traditions merely for identification with their past, or the 'back-home' feeling, etc. but the emerging generation must re-discover its original intended meaning and re-interpret its significance for the modern world. We must not get lost in the nostalgic experience of some romanticized 'perfect past' of the traditions. In the name of traditions, the immigrant generation tries to re-create their childhood family, community and faith memories, not knowing it does not give their kids the same sense of connection or meaning. Seeing the turbulence of our times and uncertainties of the future, they resort to living in the idealized past. They are trapped in a time capsule – thinking that things back home are the same as when they left it a few decades ago.

There is a pressing need for retrieval of traditions from the past and their re-appropriation for present settings. There is tremendous power to give meaning and sense of belonging in traditions. We must take the familiar practices and re-interpret them to give new meaning to the new generation. We must re-discover some of the tradition for original meaning and give them a fresh lease of life by articulating its relevancy in contemporary language. Not only do we need to redeem traditions, but we need to create new traditions as well. New traditions - isn't that an oxymoron? Is not tradition always taken from the past? Some tend to throw out the baby with the bath water. In spite of the problems traditions have caused us in the past, we need to see the

> **Do not move an ancient boundary stone set up by your forefathers.**
> **Proverbs 22:28 (NIV)**

proper place and power of traditions. Some postmodern thinkers[8] have called us to distinguish between church traditions and the Christian tradition and to move the emphasis from the former to the later. We need to gain a perspective far beyond our own denominational church practices to include and celebrate all Christian practices that has transforming potential for our constituencies, without sacrileging any particular expressions of it.

Our ability to understand the future will depend on our understanding of the past. If we do not care to learn from those who have gone before us, we are bound to make the same mistakes, and these traditions would help us in this process. We need to look into our past in order to understand how we got where we are today. We also need to study contemporary realties and together with those two trajectories, you may know what is to come. As we begin to discern the lessons from history and contours of the emerging culture, we could probably locate where the church is headed in the future.

Believe, Belong, Behave: Which Comes First?

Our traditional understanding was that an individual who is born in a Christian family/community and he/she "behaves" in a certain manner and "belongs" to the community around him which determines his religious orientation. He/she may come to personally "believe" in Christ or not, but remain a part of the church and community by virtue of his birth.

The missionary understanding was that an individual first becomes a Christian by "believing" in Jesus Christ; then he/she joins a church or a local fellowship and finds their "belonging"; They begin to imitate others around him or based on what is being taught at the church, which determines his/her "behaving".

In the former, the starting point is behavior while in the later it is belief. The process is flip-flopped. But in both cases, belonging played a central role. In either case, a sense of belonging was pivotal, no matter where you start on the journey of discovery of faith and behavior.

The problem is that believing is not enough without lifestyle transformation. External behavior modification falls far short of bringing lasting inner change. Mere cultural conditioning fails to satisfy a generation who vow their allegiance to multiple cultures.

The Coconut generation is quick to decipher the hypocritical attitude and actions of the immigrant generation. Those who have grown up in the church are frustrated with double standards of behaviors – what they see around them and what they read in the Bible. The second generation struggle to embrace a faith that has innate contradiction or lacks in its potential for total life change. They do not want to settle for anything less. They are inspired by the teachings and life of Jesus Christ and feel the tug in their hearts toward Christ, but hesitate to make a life commitment, when they see people who call themselves Christians who are unlike Christ in every way. They are looking for people who have been deeply impacted by Christ and who strive to live a Christ-like life everyday. They are looking for people for whom Jesus is real and who are honest in their faith struggles.

More recently, a softer approach is adopted by many, where belonging precedes the other two. Belonging is assumed to be a way into Christian faith. Helping young people build relationships with other peers and adults, where they feel safe, loved and affirmed – creating a sense of

> **Don't copy the behavior and customs of this world, but let God transform you into a new person by changing the way you think.**
> **Rom 12:2a (NLT)**

belonging. Then they would explore faith of those around them resulting in healthy character formation. This is a kinder, seeker-sensitive approach, where people are less judgmental and more open, interactive and supportive. The priority of belonging tends to make gatherings informal, less structured, fellowship driven, and non-hierarchical.

All this forces us to question our continuum of believe-behave-belong. What is the starting point for Coconut generation? Are there multiple starting points? Are there other components to the "be" paradigm? Should there be any starting point, at all? At a conference in July 2000, British Asian Christians (more accurately South Asian Christians in United Kingdom) met together to consider this paradigm more closely. The theme was "Belonging, Believing, Behaving: British Asian Discipleship in the 21st century". Pradip Sudra of the Evangelical Alliance made an appeal that "belonging, believing, behaving are not a single continuum where there is a definite starting point and an ending point but that the staring point for becoming a disciple of Christ can be at any of the three points."[9] But the key word here is "becoming", the forth "be" which encompasses all other three "be"s. Others call this process Christian formation, faith development, growth, or maturation.

So where is home for Coconut generation? They are in exile, awaiting arrival to a better place, where they fully belong and live forever. As sojourners, their profound quest is to be part of something bigger than themselves and everything they know of. Some fall along the journey, some settle for less or say there can be no home; but some do experience life changing encounters with the Divine and inclusion into the family of God – a home where I fully belong and nothing can disturb that sense of security.

To Ponder About:

1. What are some strengths and weakness within your community and family? How does it shape your sense of belonging?

2. How are you same or different from your parent's generation?

3. List some traditions that you see in your fellowship or church. Research into its origin, practice and meanings. Which traditions have had positive spiritual impact on you? Which traditions need to be redeemed and how would you do it?

4. What major changes are happening around you: personal life, family, church, neighborhood, culture and the world? How would you use the anchor of tradition through the turbulence?

5. What connection do you see "believe, behave, belong" in your life? How is it different in others you know?

Endnotes

[1] Jhumpa Lahiri's interview with *New Yorker* magazine after the release of her second novel *Namesake*. She was awarded a 2000 Pulitzer Prize for her *Interpreter of Maladies*, (New York: Houghton Mifflin Co, 1999).

[2] Means Family in Hindi.

[3] Peter Benson, *The Troubled Journey,* (Minneapolis: Search Institute, 1990) 7.

[4] Peter Drucker, *The Post-Capitalist Society* (New York: Harper Collins, 1993) 1.

[5] Means Community in Sanskrit, Hindi and other Indian languages.

[6] John Ortberg, *Everybody is Normal Till You Get To Know Them,* (Grand Rapids: Zondervan, 2003) 40.

[7] Means Tradition in Sanskrit, Hindi and other Indian languages.

[8] Leonard Sweet, Brian McLaren, Sally Morgenthaler etc. have written on the differences.

[9] *Jewels In His Crown* conference (London, UK, July 2000) 19-20.

6

Beyond Denial:
Unearthing Struggles of Coconuts

Our youths have bad manners, contempt for authority;
They show disrespect for their elders; they no
longer rise when elders enter the room.
They contradict their parents, gobble up their food
and tyrannize their teachers.
– Socrates, 5ᵗʰ century B.C.

Until a couple of decades ago, we thought it was safe to bury toxic industrial wastes. But now we have learned it doesn't just go away - it leaks into the water table, destroys the soil, and infects the crops. As the contamination moves along the food supply chain, it eventually affects human beings and our entire world. Burying past hurts and grief does the same thing. We all have learned it, sometimes in the hard way, that shoving things under the rug is a very poor solution to the problems in life. The passage of time doesn't heal them and the pain does not simply disappear. In fact, it begins to hurt all the more over time and makes us incapable to exhume or face them. Buried pain leaks into our emotional system and wreaks havoc there. It distorts our perceptions of life, and it taints our relationships. This subconscious contamination destroys families, churches and communities.

A common response, particularly relevant among Indian societies, is the undeniable fact of denial. When ignoring does not work, deny them categorically. Even when the problem is staring at us and is obvious to all, we put up a brave front and boldly declare it to the world that it does not exist at all. The parents think that their kids are the best kids in the world – this is more than parental pride, but using them to advance their own standing in the society. The next generation has become so adept in handling multiple masks that they feel lost behind the many cover-ups. The perception of others, communal morals, experience of shame, etc. contribute to the problem of denial.

Over the last couple of years, I asked youth leaders and pastors of the Indian American community to list their top crises issues that the second generation is facing. With such an open ended question, you can imagine, I received many interesting responses. Although we have covered many fundamental questions of their uniqueness in the previous chapters, I want to raise some pressing matters prevalent with this generation. This is not to wash dirty linen in public, but to confront the hard realities before this generation head-on rather than running away from them. We cannot understand a generation without knowing their pain and struggles. Some of the issues are more widespread than others and some affect very few people in the populace. But it is laid out here in order for us to come to terms with the real challenges facing our communities and hopes that we become agents of healing and restoration in our community.

Moreover, most of these issues listed below are symptomatic and some are inter-related. The real issues are buried deep under multiple layers and unearthing is hard work and seeking healing is even harder. A deeper understanding of Indian culture will help us to grasp the depth of these complexities. I have described seven major struggles, not in any order and it includes some related issues as well. Also I would not have the time or space to expand on each of the issues and its far-reaching implications. This chapter only permits a surface level treatment and we encourage you to seek professional help and look for available resources in your neighborhood and church.

1. Isolation: Home Alone

The Coconut generation find themselves distant from their parent's generation and from mainstream Americans as well. This extreme sense of exclusion is called double marginalization – first on account of ethnicity and secondly, due to generational differences. Josh McDowell called the generation born and raised through the 80's and 90's the 'Disconnected Generation'[1]. The struggle of immigrant parents, both of whom often work outside of home and/or multiple shifts, is leaving the second generation in the care of older siblings, television, or in "cheap" child care arrangements. How the second generation was raised, their values and priorities of their parents cast a long shadow on their progenies. Their social skills are modest and prevailing racial prejudices further aggravates the sense of loneliness.

Mother Teresa called loneliness "the leprosy of modern society." Nobody wants anyone else to know that they're a leper, even as it destroys them gradually. The sense of isolation is eating up this generation from within and sadly adult care-givers have no clue about the extent of this problem. George Gallup described Americans as the "loneliest people on earth", and I think children of the recent immigrants would stand on top of that list.

In the survey, many Indian American youth leaders confirmed a deep sense of loneliness faced by their youths. Most kids are left to deal with isolation on their own by filling the void with lesser things. The party or clubbing culture of the Coconut generation is indicative of this. The Coconut generation is desperately searching for trustworthy and abiding friendships to diminish their sense of loneliness. They long for fellowship and the company of other sojourners like them or others who genuinely care for them with no ulterior motives. Many youth leaders recommended deliberately incorporating extended times of fellowship in their ministries with the Coconut generation. "They love hanging out together... enjoying the presence of each other ... so we should not rush into worship or teaching or activities. *Koinonia* (Biblical word of fellowship) meets a deep need in Coconut generation and we should be intentional about it."

For youth today, the internet is not simply for emailing and browsing on the web for information, but it is used for instant messaging, chat rooms and blogs as an attempt to connect with others out there, who are like them. When one generation uses the internet for information, the emerging generation uses it for relationship.

A youth leader once told me about his attempt to get into the instant messaging buddy list of all his kids in the youth group. "I generally try to be online when my youths are online. You never know when they need you. But whenever that happens, they know whom to contact." That is a great way to address the needs of loneliness and being there for the kids in their desperate moments.

2. Sex: Sshhh!

Sex is a taboo topic in the Asian Indian community; no one dares to speak openly about it, but everyone is expected to adhere to traditional conservative ways. But coming to American has changed all that. Far too many young people are having sex before they graduate from high school. The Coconut generation is often told repeatedly, "How could you go to college without 'experiencing' it? If you are still a virgin, everyone looks down on you. What's wrong with you? Everyone is doing it." Our young people experience intense peer pressure to be sexually active and they have no one to turn to for help and support. Parents, pastors and other adults who have never been exposed to the American school/college culture are clueless about these pervasive influences and do not know how to appropriately help.

This is a generation in which sexual frankness has become a permanent feature of the landscape, with uncertain long-term implications. The media, particularly Internet has made explicit images more accessible to more people at younger ages. Many youth leaders have admitted that a good number of young men in their groups have regularly raised questions about pornography. Whether they look for it or not, sexually explicit content is thrown at them almost everyday. The massive spillover of sexually charged materials into the mainstream and the prevailing cultural norms of adults in our community leaves our young people disillusioned on matters of sexuality and morality.

In the survey, youth leaders across the country confirmed that sexual sin and sexual abuse are all too common in the Indian American community. This generation believes that sexual behavior is merely a matter of personal choice; no one else has the right to meddle with it. They are turning less to adults or religion for values or sexual mores and turning more to peers and media for determining appropriate sexual practices. They feel it is their right to engage sexually, and it is sometimes seen as being trendy to their American counterparts. Once a young lady told me, "I just need to be careful not to get pregnant; that is too much of a hassle. What if family and community finds out about it? If you do get pregnant, of course there is a solution – get an abortion. I had to get it once."

Another young lady shared her sexual history not so long ago, "I first had sex when I was 15 at a friend's party with a guy I had come to know just that evening. We both were drunk and I hated the experience ever since. Then I went away to college and started dating guys regularly; I had many boyfriends and kept having sex with many of them. Of course none of this behavior was sanctioned by my family, community or faith, so I had to keep it under cover. After I moved to another city for graduate studies, I got serious with Jesus and made a vow to abstain from casual sex. That went quite well, until I met this guy, whom I thought I will get married to – I had sex at his apartment and then he broke up with me. That really hurt me bad; I thought we were in a "committed relationship" and had even talked about marriage. It is so frustrating; I hope to be chaste until I meet the guy I get married to."

Coconut men equally struggle in this area and there are growing levels of promiscuity across denominations and faith groups. Sometimes talks on modesty, abstinence, and sexual purity are rejected as "Indian ways", especially when it comes from their parents, like everything else. One of the most popular series of talks that my wife and I have done for many youth groups in the country is the one on "love, sexuality and marriage". In spite of the prevailing confusion on the subject, this generation is hungry to learn what God has to say in this matter. Instead of what culture says or what our traditions are, we have to take them into scriptures to discover God as the one who created sex, who is the source of all love and who instituted marriage.

3. Past hurts: Digging Deep

Indian American young people are adept at putting up a brave front. But behind the "picture-perfect" faces and "prime-time camera-ready" poses, there are many deep hurts – physical, emotional and sexual. They often shove them under the rug, thinking that they will go away or time will heal. Their attempts to cover things up is also due to their inability to correctly locate what is really causing the pain, failure to articulate their hurts, and not knowing where to go for help. Having grown up in dysfunctional family situations, they carry the scars of verbal abuse and emotional hurts from their early years. Alcoholic parents, abusive adults, hurtful sarcasm are all too common in many Indian-American homes. Some have been physically and sexually abused by parents, relatives, cousins or neighbors. Some are struggling with past broken relationships, sexual fantasies, pornography, rape, abortion, etc. and feel too delicate even to broach these struggles with anyone. Some exhibit homosexual tendencies and feel 'weird' about themselves. Most importantly, they suffer the pain all alone, often thinking there is no one to turn to.

I have had young men confide to me how they discovered their parent's extra-marital relationships and addiction to pornography. Such double standards of adults leave the young people confused, angry and wanting to 'run away' from home and their parents. Many have bad memories of their early childhood, even in cases of normal upbringing, that continue to haunt them through adolescent years and well into their adulthood. They suffer neglect and rejection on account of parent's busyness and preoccupation with careers, interests and travels.

The traditional Indian-style parenting sometimes hurls verbal abuses on young tender Coconuts and physically beat them up in the name of discipline. Growing up in homes where fathers were alcoholic and, under the influence, turn abusive to their wives and children is all too common in Indian American homes. Some have grown up in homes where parents don't get along and habitually quarrel over petty matters. All of which makes the second generation bitter, angry and frustrated. The prolonged internment of these feelings without any help erodes these young people completely over time.

Even those who are active in church and youth leadership

have their own dark corners. After I had developed a trusting relationship with one of the youth leaders, I was shocked at the 'skeletons' hidden in his 'attic'. He has never dealt with his past and has been suffering from extreme self-condemnation. Through repeated replays, these negative emotions and past hurts keep haunting him. Cleaning up dark corners of our lives, sharing our own struggles from the past and being honest about it, really helps. Of course, unconditional acceptance and love help the attic cleaning process and being whole again.

4. Finding A Life Partner: *Shaadi or Barbadi*[2]

Most Indian parents wish their children would marry within their own 'kind.' The out-marriage (marrying outside of one's race and religion) is strongly disapproved across most ethnic Indian churches, but they are on a steady rise. Their resistance to western assimilation and cultural superiority of Indian ways are obviously some of the reasons. They hold the view that Indian marriages are better and fear divorce of their children. But there is more to it than what is noticeable otherwise. The characteristics of Indian Americans who outmarry are: second generation or later, born in the west, female, older, better educated, of higher occupational status, and have higher income.

Like every other immigrant community in America, the emerging generation of Indians has also married outside their race and religion. The perception of Coconut generation varies in regard to out-marriages. The assimilation matrix section in the Authentic Hybrid chapter (Figure 4.1), we discussed some of their views on marital relationships.

Matters get worse, as in the Indian social system where parents are expected to find a match for their children. No matter how successful one is in his/her profession or business, if they are not able to find a suitable match for their children, they are considered as a failure. The parents of marriageable children constantly face questions from fellow immigrants and feel a sense of shame in the community. The power dynamics of Indian family systems, particularly in-law relationships further enhance this notion, where mothers gain more influence by having a son or a daughter-in-law and having grandsons.

The young Indian women will continue to face difficulty in finding Indian mates for a variety of reasons. The current gender ratio of Coconut generation is tilted toward women – (there are 114 women for every 100 men between the ages of 15 and 24). The 'never married' population of Asian Indians is 26.7% and separated and divorced adds up to 3.3% of the entire population above the age of 15[3]. In the Christian circles, although there are no statistical data available, trends are higher than the average. Generally men who have grown up in America are open to marrying girls from India, but the reverse is less likely. Depending on assimilation patterns Coconut women hold many stereotypes about Indian men and are not willing to become the traditional Indian *"bahu"*. When American born Indian men get married to girls from India or from outside of the community, the case becomes even more difficult for girls to find a match within the community. The marriageable young women outnumber men 2:1 in most churches. When we add Christian commitment and ministry involvements, that ratio goes as high as 6:1 (i.e. women: men)[4] in some circles.

In the years to come, out-marriages are bound to increase and some will choose to remain single. Our churches and communities will be forced to reconcile with this fact. A pastor admitted to me, "When one of our youth leaders got married outside the church to a white American, we saw a series of marriages outside the community and there was a mass exodus of our young people on account of out-marriages."

I asked him, "Why don't they stay in the church with their non-Indian spouses?"

"Our adults don't want that. They want to maintain cultural and ethnic homogeneity in the church. They experience the shame of having failed to preserve the community ideals and are ostracized because others don't want their children to follow their steps. So they try to keep away all non-conforming elements." This is a major tug-of-war between expectations of parents/community and figuring out God's will amidst the bleaker prospects of finding a spouse and is a real challenge in ministry to the emerging generations.

5. Low Self Worth: Short on Value

Having grown up as children of immigrant families in a foreign culture, the Coconuts suffer from a very stunted view of themselves. They feel torn between two worlds; that is exactly what happens to their self – a tear, which is sometimes stitched or held together; others patch up their self to cover the tear. But what they cannot do is to feel the way it used to be or whole. A tear is a permanent part of their self and causes them to feel something is fundamentally wrong with them.

The crisis is aggravated as this generation is growing up in America, where the self esteem movement is so widespread and high self esteem is considered a necessity to succeed. A profound sense of marginality, identity confusion, uprootedness, and lack of strong friendships further contributes to this problem. Parental neglect or ignorance and absence of significant adults leaves them with none to speak words of wisdom, encouragement, guidance and affirmation. Once a youth leader in Florida told me, "Their sense of self is at dangerously low levels; they are running on empty tanks. I have become intentional to affirm and encourage them. Sometimes they are surprised to hear such things from me. No one else speaks to them like that." May this "Baranabas" tribe increase!

Some clear indications of low self worth among Coconut generation are the signs of depression. Most teenagers disguise it; some are not able to do so anymore. Some suffer occasional bouts of it, and for others it is a constant companion. It often gets overlooked as teenage moodiness or as a result of hormonal changes. In some cases the depression comes on suddenly or creeps in over a period of days or weeks and could gradually slide into deeper problems, like suicidal tendencies. Matters get further complicated when young people attempt unhealthy ways to cope with their struggles.

Contrary to popular belief, young people are looking for authority figures. When existing authority figures enforce themselves, the youth rebel against them. With this generation, authority cannot be demanded; it must be earned. After many failed attempts in building trustworthy relationships with others, they have developed a cocooned mentality. They are looking for someone who is worthy of their trust, one who is authentic and someone who will genuinely care for them. Some demand authority on account of a position or title that one holds such as parent, pastor, youth leader etc., which does not mean much to the youth these days. They are quick to decipher power plays, political maneuvering, cultural cover-ups and manipulation attempts and they outrightly reject them.

Asian Indian youths struggle not only with the color of their skin, but also their bodies and features. Differences between Indian appearence and their American peers along with popular media further aggravate this crisis. Image and physical appearance are extremely important to all teenagers as they compare themselves with others. They want to look like their favorite movie stars, sports figures and pop idols that they see on television and Internet. According to one study, rising levels of eating disorders, bulimia, depression, and even suicidal tendencies in Asian Indian teenage girls is the result of poor body image, a distorted view of beauty, and lack of relational skills. [5]

This generation is pushing the limits on clothing, fashion, hairstyles, modesty, image consciousness, expressions of sexuality, etc. They are trying to define themselves by imitating popular icons, and in the absence of proper role models in the Indian American community, they end up aping mostly Western trends. Also this is an attempt to distance themselves from their parent's 'style' of clothing and fashion. However, in recent years, with the growing popularity of Indian cinema in the West and rise of global beauty queens from India, many Indian American youths consider it to be 'cool' to mimic Indian fashion symbols.

Both Asian Indian young men and women suffer from this problem. Men worry about how tall, strong or big they are. The worst thing for men is probably being short and skinny; they have bought into the "tall, dark, and handsome" myth. In the youth survey many youth leaders agreed to dangerous levels of obsession with physical appearance among both young men and women in this generation. Peer pressure to conform to some expected standards are intense among this generation and most adults are naïve about this insidious influence.

Much more is at stake for young women in matters of body image. Mary Pipher writes that "America is a 'girl-poisoning, girl-destroying culture. She outlines the manner in which, early in adolescence, girls are called on to sacrifice their authentic selves and trade spontaneity and honesty for disorientation and depression. Girls today are growing up in a 'more dangerous, sexualized and media saturated culture. They face incredible

124

pressure to be beautiful and sophisticated, which in junior high means using chemicals and being sexual. As they navigate a more dangerous world, girls are less protected."[6]

"Emphasis on inner beauty and how to cultivate that is a strong emphasis in our girls group" tells a lady youthworker in Boston. "They need to know that they are deeply loved of God and we need to accept them, no matter how they look or what they wear or what they are going through."

6. Addictions: Hooked On

The survey confirmed that Indian American young people are struggling with all sorts of addictions – alcohol, materialism, drugs, gambling, sex, pornography etc. Some feel so trapped in it and think that there is no way out of it. They want to get out it, but do not know how. Nobody seems to understand their dilemma or seems to care. Parents and religious leaders tend to condemn them or offer simplistic solutions, exposing their ignorance to the complexity of the problem.

Addiction is a state of powerlessness and the inability to manage one's life because of a physical or emotional dependence on an outside agent. Teenagers normally delight in trying new things and the most alluring experimentation is with forbidden things. And doing it under the cover of parents and keeping it from them enhances the enjoyment. The casual drinking to occasional use of alcohol or drugs soon escalate to desperate dependence. The party or clubbing culture among Indian American youths is often a great starting place for experimenting with alcohol and drugs. As they go away to college, freed from the clutches of parents and their domineering presence into the college dorms where alcohol flows freely, things takes a turn for the worse.

An Asian Indian campus worker in the West Coast once told me, "They are trying to fill the emptiness they are feeling with bottles, crack and cocaine. Many Indian kids come from extremely controlling and manipulative home environments and they swing to other extremes at college. They experiment with everything out there and in the process without their knowledge find themselves dependent on substances."

A community-wide addiction for Asian Indians is materialism, and they tend to overdo it having achieved relatively high success in America. The Coconut generation has grown up with more toys, more television, and more "stuff" than their parents back in India. They have been ingrained with a materialistic and consumeristic mindset right from their homes. Yet, they are deeply aware of how more "stuff" in life does not satisfy their deepest longing.

What the problem of addiction really needs is intensive discipleship. The addicts need to get hooked on something more powerful that can turn their lives upside-down and inside-out. "Putting the cork on the bottle (not using drugs or alcohol) is no guarantee of any lasting change in an individual's life. What addicts need is a systematic commitment to an ongoing process of personal spiritual growth. Christian recovery means gaining new tools that enable us to live a new sober life and to remove all the "stumbling blocks" to victorious life for rest of their lives." Wise words indeed!

7. Fear: *Dar aur Dard*[7]

Believe it or not, Asian Indian young people in America are fearful. The results of the online survey coincided with what many youth leaders have known intuitively for a long time. This generation is fearful of many things and for many reasons. They exhibit signs of fear about the future and fear of failing to live up to the expectation of their parents. Immigrant parents set overly ambitious dreams, which they vicariously live out through their children in education, career, lifestyle, success, money etc. These expectations are far beyond the reach that young people think they could achieve. As the Asian Indian immigrant in America falls among the most educated and wealthiest, the pressure to succeed academically and later financially is intense on the second generation. The fear of failure almost incapacitates them from experiencing normal adolescent lives. They even torment themselves through psychological self flagellation as they feel they have disappointed their parents.

Children rarely question their parents' expectations, but instead question their own personal inadequacy. As ambitious immigrants with an insatiable appetite for wealth, prominence and power, they set almost unfathomable goals for their children: grades they must maintain, Ivy League schools they should attend, professions they should choose, careers and businesses they should pursue, and spouse they should marry. Often this pressure is associated with an ulterior motive to advance their own status in the society on account of their children's success. Some parents try to live out the American dream through their children, what they could not actualize for themselves. They are unaware of the pain that it languishes upon their children. The fear of failing to achieve parent's expectation is often greater than failure itself.

Coconuts constantly live with fear of relationships, fear of commitment and fear of transparency. What if I do not find love? Will I be forced to marry someone? What if I am not happy in my marriage? To whom can I bare my soul? They also show fear of exposure – what happens when people find out about the real me? This anxiety causes them to tightly hold on to all the cover-ups.

Going Beyond Denial: Whole Again

All of these pressing issues of the Coconut generation need to be studied at length from its unique religio-cultural context and appropriate help made available to the community. If you are or someone you know is struggling with these or other crisis issues, I strongly encourage you to seek professional help. There are many other issues that we could cover here like dating, broken relationships, adultery, violent behaviors, gangs, felony, homosexuality, children of divorce etc. that are prevalent in growing measure in the emerging generation of Indian Americans.

A promising sign that I see in the Indian American community is the growing number of young people who are pursuing higher education in mental health sciences, psychology and pastoral counseling. One doctoral psychology student once confessed to me, "I pursued this field to seek healing in my own life. Without that I could never help others; but my experiences have given me a passion to feel deeply about issues and empathize with hurting people in my community." I am hopeful that their knowledge and skill with a generational commitment, will serve hurting Coconuts and our churches well. May this tribe grow and provide much needed ministry to our community.

Some of the problems the Coconut generation faces can be traced back to the previous generations, where someone opened the door to a sinful lifestyle, demonic influences, spiritual bondages etc. Youth leaders must discern generational and spiritual bondages associated with sinful behavior patters, such as lying, cheating, anger, immorality, workaholism and materialism. Not only can generational sins ruin our lives, but may continue to affect our descendants.

We must get beyond the denial phase to confront these hard

realities head-on. Admission of the problem is half way to recovery, while denial only multiplies the woes. We need to move from a legalistic community to a grace-giving community; committed to wholeness and nurturing others towards wholeness. Jesus promises us "life in all its fullness" (John 10:10). We must celebrate the abundant life and become agents of hope and recovery in the Indian American community. A community is only as strong as its weakest member and with the alarming levels of hurt and pain among the emerging generation of Asian Indians, these issues need to be taken up more seriously or else the entire generation and the church will weaken its witness in the world.

To Ponder About:

1. List some issues that you know Coconut generation is struggling with. How do you deal with them?

2. What keeps this generation from seeking help? Identify obstacles facing them.

3. What help is available in your church, campus and neighborhood for pressing issues of the Coconut generation?

4. How can you be more aware, educated and equipped to handle these and other crises?

5. What could you do change the culture of denial in our community and raise agents of healing and hope in the Asian Indian American community?

Endnotes

[1] Josh McDowell, *Disconnected Generation: Saving our Youth from Self Destruction,* (Nashville: Word Publishing, 2000).

[2] Means Wedding or Destruction in Hindi.

[3] Taken from the US Census Bureau Report "We the People – Asians in the US" from US census bureau. (www.census.org)

[4] These figures are based on an informal survey. No statistical study has been done in this area.

[5] I am grateful to Sheryl Sasi for her unpublished study of teenage girls in Indian American congregations in Chicago, 2002.

[6] Mary Pipher, *Reviving Ophelia: Saving the Selves of Adolescent Girls,* (New York: Ballantine Books, 1995) 13.

[7] Means Fear and Pain in Hindi.

7

Faith Matters:
Spirituality & Church of Coconuts

The destiny of the world hinges on the church's
dialogue with the cultures of our time.
– Pope John Paul II

The great evangelist D.L. Moody once sent a group of people out to witness in the city of Chicago. One man came back to report that two and a half people had become Christians. "Two and a half people, what do you mean by that?" Moody asked.

"Oh, it's simple. There were two adults and an eleven year old boy - he's the half."

"If you want to keep statistics like that you've got it backwards." Moody said. "The one-half would be the adults, because half of their lives are gone. The boy has his whole life ahead of him to live for Jesus Christ." Moody understood the priority of reaching the next generation.

It is unfortunate that many in the Indian church do not see youth ministry as real ministry. I came to a personal relationship with Christ in my mid-teens at a point of committing suicide, and I always had a heart for young people. There is something about being young and their quest for God that I simply cannot have enough of. Although I am involved in a variety of different ministries these days, youthwork is still my first love. I find myself gravitating towards ministry with the emerging generation, almost unconsciously. Statistics tells us that most people come to receive Christ personally into their lives in their teen years and I believe the most important ministry of Christianity is with the young people. The evangelist Billy Graham said that Christianity is only a generation away from extinction; the coming generation could be the one.

A common misconception in the Indian community is that engaging in ministry to the youth is somehow less than full-fledged Christian ministry. It is obvious from the fact that very few Indian churches have assigned staff to nurture the spiritual needs of the emerging generations. Most immigrant churches are single staff organizations who in most cases have generalist that takes the overall responsibility of the congregation with the help of volunteer committees. Amidst the busyness of shepherding the flock (which is overwhelming in itself), the Coconut generation falls through the cracks, hemorrhaging profusely!

Diaspora Faith: Transplanted Communities

The sociology of religions informs us that religious institutions have played an indispensable role in immigrant adaptation by facilitating the creation of community, construction of ethnic identity, and transmission of homeland culture and values to children.[1] As the Indians were scattered around the world, they took their faith with them, including specific beliefs, rituals and traditions, in spite of the prohibition against crossing "the black waters" in the ancient Indian writings. Religion became a crucial element of the global Indian Diaspora experience. Their faith accompanied them and vibrant religious communities were established wherever they went. Transplantation is an apt metaphor – they uproot themselves and transported to a distant land and were planted in a new, often dissimilar soil; yet they flourished everywhere.

Globally, Indian Diaspora built temples, mosques, *gurudwaras* and churches to gather together, to promote faith practices and in order to preserve their religious and cultural identity. It has also helped them to maintain a strong link to India and continuity with their home culture overseas. Modern transportation, telecommunication, and economic prosperity have aided those aspirations.

Indians in America belong to a wide range of faith traditions, probably more diverse than any other immigrant community, as India is home of many religious systems and migration occurred across the entire religious spectrum. Although Hinduism is the faith of the majority of people in India, it sometimes mistakenly includes animists, tribal religions and even faith traditions that sprung from Hinduism like Buddhism, Sikhism, Jainism, etc. Most of the first wave of immigrants who came to America in the early twentieth century, were called 'Hindoos', albeit a small fraction were followers of Hinduism. One-third was Muslims and the majority was Sikhs.[2]

As the Indian immigrant population began to grow in the United States in the 70's and 80's, they came together on weekends and holidays for informal fellowship and to celebrate their cultural and religious heritage. The pioneering spirit of the Indian immigrants is clearly evident in matters of faith. Even as they were getting rooted in this "foreign" land, they quickly built their religious establishments. It was not only representative of their religiosity, but also an attempt to preserve their culture and to transmit their values effectively to the coming generations. Indian-American Hindus become more religious and nationalistic in the United

States[3]. Indian Christians, on the other hand, found it easier than others because of many active churches and Christian ministries in America. They could easily rent church facilities to conduct worship services and communal rituals and took advantage of various Christian ministries.

The majority of Indian Americans today are Hindus, and there are over 500 Hindu temples scattered all across the United States[4]. Hinduism was first introduced to the United States by Swami Vivekananda, a young intellectual religious leader who represented India to the World Parliament of Religions in Chicago in 1893. The number of Indian mosques is difficult to determine, as most Indian Muslims worship along with Muslims of other ethnicities. A fewer number of Sikh *Gurudwaras* and Jain Temples can be seen in most big cities of America. In addition, there are numerous Indian religious and charitable societies, educational, social and cultural organizations engaged in a variety of causes and activities.

The ethnic Indian churches in America come in all sizes and shapes. They are divided along the lines of language, culture, denomination and doctrine. In the early days, when numbers were smaller, they met together in spite of differences in language, denominational affiliations and even doctrines. As more people arrived, they began forming their own congregations and building their own churches. According to some estimates there are currently over 800 Indian churches in America. It could be as high as 1000 churches[5]. The earliest registered Indian church in America was established in 1971 in New York by the Indian Orthodox Christians[6], although some home fellowships and congregations can be dated earlier.

Throughout the 1970s and 80s, there was a proliferation of Indian churches in major cities of America. These churches conduct regular Sunday services in many languages like Bengali, Gujarati,

Hindi, Kanada, Malayalam, Punjabi, Tamil, Telugu, etc. This perfectly fits within the prevailing American religious landscape. America is a segregated society along the lines of ethnicity and race and this is no more evident than on Sunday mornings – the most segregated hour of the week. About 90% of American religious organizations are comprised of at least 90% of one racial group.[7] It encourages separate ethnic religious gatherings, even when the tenets of the faith are universalistic and ecumenical. They remain ethnically exclusive in their church while adhering to a more inclusive global faith.

The non-Christian Indians, particularly Hindus, view Christians as having departed from their historic Indian culture. They view Christianity as a Western religion and all followers of Christianity are opposed to traditional Indian ways. What they are unaware of is the fact that Christianity came to India far before the West was even discovered! The common stereotype is that all Indians are Hindus. Navin talked about the racial slur that was used against him, "They painted 'Hindu' on my car. I was pretty annoyed at first. Not everyone from India is a Hindu. Hinduism is a religion, not a race. I'm a Christian, actually. My entire family has been Christians for generations. But they see you and they think, 'Hindu.' I know what they are trying to say by using that term. It is a mean and ignorant thing to do."

Indian Immigrant Churches: What's Right/What's Wrong?

Indian Christians have shown remarkable pioneering spirit in starting so many churches all across the adopted land of America. Even when ecclesiastical authorities in India were opposed to starting Indian parishes in a "Christian country," the immigrant Indian Christians in major metropolitan cities persevered in sustaining small gatherings that met periodically for worship and for a sense of community.[8] Most Indian congregations were established with their own lay initiative, meager resources, and without much support from American churches. Almost all of Indian congregations are organized along the lines of ethnicity, language and doctrinal traditions.

Most Indian church growth happens as a result of immigration and biological growth. Some are closed to having Indian converts from other religions or other Christians from other races. Most Indian American churches are ingrown, self satisfied, complacent, and keep their congregation from looking to the lost and needy world, both in the neighborhood and around the world. Often the idea of missionary work held by Indian pastors is limited to social work among rural or poor folks back in India. Most members of the congregation are ignorant of the missional purpose of the church.[9]

The Christianity of many of the Indian churches makes it difficult to draw the line between culture and faith. They practice a culturalized Christianity, invariably propagating Indian culture in the name of God. It is often done unconsciously and is evident across linguistic, ethnic, doctrinal, and denominational lines. The church becomes the socialization vehicle to nurture the next generation in the culture and not necessarily biblical faith. Sometimes behaving the Indian way takes precedence over the Christian or even the Biblical way. Sometimes it is reinforced in the name of tradition and with unflinching zeal to preserve it from adulteration from American Christianity.

Such churches will survive and even prosper if immigration continues. Nevertheless, they will face major struggles in retaining the young who have grown up within their churches. The contributing factors of this challenge surfaced in a recent discussion with a denominational church minister. Apart from the obvious exodus of young people from our churches as they move to other cities for study or work, there is also a decline in church participation by the younger generation. The reasons he cited include materialism, pride, failure to appreciate Indian religious practices, the intergenerational gulf, sensuality, media, narcissism etc.

Most Indian church leaders have not realized the complexities of the Indian American mind and do not understand why the second generation acts the way they do. Some try to assert their authority and demand unquestioned obedience. Often they lack the skill, patience, willingness to learn, understand, and hence effectively minister to the needs of the Coconut generation. The shortsighted approach is further driving a wedge between the generations, and the church's failure is evident from the increasing dropout rate of this generation from the immigrant churches.

The signs of graying of the Indian American church are apparent everywhere. The pioneering immigrants of the 70's are approaching retirement and many are relocating to other parts of America and in some cases back to India. In recent years, there has been a trend for early retired immigrants to move to places with warmer weather, find cheaper cost of living, or live with their children. With this next wave of displacement, the earlier immigrant churches are seeing a sharp drop in church attendance and in some cases forced to re-evaluate ministry to the Coconut generation more closely.

A few years ago, I analyzed the membership pattern of couple of churches of its membership and studied church attendance over a period of time, and some interesting facts emerged. The second generation is less involved in the affairs of the church, contributes less time and money than their parents. They exhibit less ownership, and attendance of some age groups are dangerously low. If we extrapolate these trends, by the 2010 or so, most of the immigrant generation who established these churches will retire and the church's earning will plunge significantly (as much as 70% in one case).

The Indian churches in America have failed to engage with realities of the host culture. They have remained inward looking and are found fighting amongst themselves over petty matters. The ethnic Indian Church leadership failed in critical contextualization and relevancy of ministry to the emerging generation. The ethnocentric nature of Indian churches needs a conversion, like that of Peter in Acts 10, whose perception, which was characteristic of the people of his time and early Christianity, was centered on Jewish ethnicity. We could call Peter a cultural chauvinist or a benign racist. Despite of the inroad that the gospel had made among Gentiles, Peter was still an ethnocentric Christian. Likewise, although in America, immigrant Indians are still not in America. What makes Indian churches distinct is that they have been remarkably successful in re-creating the 'home' culture in the new world. Ethnocentricity is the strength and the weakness of the Indian churches.

This is a strange dilemma. The emerging generation of Indian churches in America is trying to free Christianity from Indian cultural coverings, while the emerging churches in India are trying to get rid of the Western cultural baggage. Both are striving to arrive at the "core of Christianity"[10] and have much to learn from each other. This is the challenge of critical contextualization and marks Christianity distinct from other religions.

Many Indian churches suffer from 'people blindness' – this disease keeps us from seeing the cultural distinctions of a group of people. The differences tend to create the barriers to acceptance of the message of Jesus Christ. The differences will include generational, cultural, socio-economic, educational and assimilation levels. If we fail to take these differences seriously, we would completely miss the awesome opportunity to make Christ relevant to this generation and sabotage our legacy.

Coconut Faith: Growing or Shrinking?

In early childhood and preteen years, Coconuts go to church because their parents take them there. They have no choice in this matter. Even if parents were nominal Christians, they sincerely desire that their children grow up in a religious setting.

Faith is more caught than taught.

Some parents simply shuttle kids back and forth from Sunday school and never participate in any church activities for themselves - much like any sporting or cultural activity at school or local club. Their primary hope is not that they will learn to follow Christ, but they will pick Indian ways and religious culture. They are often compared to their peers from church in matters of academic, performance, and achievement. Some Sunday schools also provide classes in Indian languages, art forms, and other cultural expressions.

During their teenage years, Coconuts begin to question their faith, assert their preference in matters of religious activities. Either they dislike religious associations and rebel against parental pressures or else they go to church because their friends are there. But at church, they do not think they can get something out of it. A common complaint of those who have dropped out of immigrant churches is "I did not get anything out of it." Conflict over second generation autonomy abounds everywhere, but many are failing in building effective generational ministry for the lack appropriate leadership, monetary resources, organizational experience and political savvy to resolve the generational conflicts.

Both the dominant white American Churches and the transplanted Indian Churches have overlooked the ministry to the Coconut generation. The American church saw them as people who have assimilated and wanted to fit into the American society, but had failed to appreciate their ethnic roots. On the other hand the transplanted church took them as one of their kind and expected them to fit right into the home culture. Ultimately, the Coconuts suffer neglect from both ends.

A Coconut is more likely to reflect the ambience of their surrounding communities, rather than a strictly ethnic one. The extended families, friends, community, church, etc. will shape their religious affiliation.

As they go away to college, away from their home and cultural settings, there is a growing spiritual openness. However, that "openness is toward all religions", an Indian American campus ministry leader told me. He says that at his campus "students are open to Jesus, but closed to Christianity as an organized religion. The Eastern Christianity that some have grown up with, stands in stark contradiction with the Western evangelical campus movements. To reach Indian students in campus, it is vital to get Indian student leaders."

> **Don't let anyone look down on you because you are young, but set an example for the believers in speech, in life, in love, in faith and in purity.**
> **1 Timothy 4:12**

An Indian pastor recently confided to me about the Coconut generation in his church, "After they leave for college, we never see them again. They appear suddenly to be married in the church and then they disappear again." Listening to our conversation, an elder of the church joined us and commented, "they only want the church to do the ceremonial rituals – baptism (this church believes in child baptism), wedding and hopefully burial." Though sarcastic, it is often true in many cases. The Coconut generation leaves their home and church when they go away to college. Some get plugged into some campus fellowships or local church, but most stay out of Christian influences. Some may return back to the immigrant churches for their wedding. When I asked a soon-to-be-groom, why he decided to get married in his parents' church, when he himself is active in another community church, he replied, "It is more for my parent's sake and our community." In the Eastern social system, marriages are more than marrying a person, but a coming together of entire clans on both sides. Even though Coconuts feel comfortable in westernized faith practices and churches, they still go back to the Indian church for the sense of community.

What is more shocking for many Indian parents is when their children choose civil ceremonies (court marriages) over religious rituals or settle for co-habitation. They ask, "Who cares for elaborate religious weddings these days?" I was talking to a marriageable-age Coconut some time ago and he argued, "What is the idea of big ceremonies? It is atrocious wastage of money. I would rather choose to get out of debt or invest in a home. That would mean lot to our future. Why all this extravagance?"

I continued my investigation, "Tell me, what kind of wedding you would like to have? Or would you have one at all?"

"Sure, don't take me wrong. I believe wedding day is an important day in the couple's life. But I don't believe in ceremonies for the sake of it or as an expression of my parents' status in the society. It would be a joyous occasion for us and we would invite close family and friends. We would only like to have people who are known to us for while and who really care for us and our marriage."

"Fair enough" I affirmed, "but how many are there that will fit that category?"

"Some 50 people!"

"That's all. Wouldn't both of your families alone make that up?" I asked knowing that both their parents have many siblings all over North America.

"Just because they are related to us does not entitle them to come for our wedding. This is our wedding, not our parents' big family get-together! I want people who are going to be involved in our lives even after the wedding; we want to share our joy with people who really matter to us. Not the cousins I have never seen or really known. Some friends are closer than a brother, you know."

This mindset is increasingly typical for many Coconuts. Dispersion of blood-relatives and less frequent interaction within their own families of origin have caused them to form surrogate families of close friends, school mates, neighbors and church community. This young man started with monetary and pragmatic reasons for a small wedding and gradually moved to deeper reasons for asserting his individuality and relationships based on choice, not blood.

The experiences of growing up in transplanted Indian community churches are diverse. For some it provided a strong sense of rootedness of their faith, balancing American socialization in schools with celebration of their ethnicity in church. But for the vast majority, Indian church was burdensome and reminds them of pain, frustration, and disappointment.

Many Coconuts are suspicious of organized religion and the institutional church. They see Sunday worship as lifeless, boring and irrelevant to their daily lives. Some withdraw from all compromised and corrupted churches into a purely private religious life. Others join small groups of "real" Christians outside or within the church whose religious experience is like their own and who share their particular understanding of authentic biblical Christian faith and life.

Some Coconuts tend to reject historical denominationalism and all restrictive central authority, and attempt to lead a life of following Jesus, seeking a more effective missional lifestyle. The rise of independent Bible or community churches are all too familiar in most cities of America and these are increasingly attracting people of Indian origin, particularly the Coconut generation. The new breed of churches and home church movement is gaining ground over traditional denominations and are proving to have appeal to Coconuts. Increasing numbers of American evangelical churches are now targeting Asian Indians and have been quite successful in drawing disenfranchised Coconuts.

Youth culture expert Kenda Dean observes, "Young people are among God's most forthright, frustrating and often unwitting prophets, reminding us that salvation is at stake, for they will not give up on love until they find it or until consumer culture numbs them into a kind of lobotomized compliance, whichever comes first. Whether they discover the true source of passion - whether they ever connect their desire for love with the life, death and resurrection of Jesus Christ or with the church at all, for that matter - largely depends on whether the church bears witness to a love more true than those available in popular culture. And that of course depends on whether the church practices the passion we preach....Passionless Christianity has nothing to die for: it practices assimilation, not oddity. Passionless Christians lead sensible lives, not subversive ones; we are benignly nice instead of dangerously loving."[11]

Coconut Spirituality: Fresh Brook or Arid Desert

The second generation spirituality stands out clearly, if you are careful to notice them. At its core, it reveals a hybrid nature, freely borrowing from all that they are exposed to. The younger leaders try to fuse what they perceive to be essential beliefs, symbols and practices from a variety of cultural and spiritual resources available to them like Indian thought, immigrant Protestantism, American evangelicalism and Spirit-led Pentecostalism.

"My generation is discontent with dead religion," said a Coconut youth leader in San Francisco, "Our generation wants a tangible experience of God who is real." Somehow faith is not real in church and they see their parent's church packed with hypocrites. They have seen it through and through and some have created a deep repulsiveness to it. The options before them are obvious: they will pursue their idealism and seek other communities of faith, start church that reflects their spirituality and passion, or give up God completely. What the youth leader did know was that the institutional church wasn't attuned to the world he lived in. He has concluded that the church is closed to theological engagement and equally incapable to respond to the challenge of a postmodern culture in which institutional authority, absolute truth, and even a rationalistic world view no longer hold sway.

Coconuts are rejecting Christianity as it was for their parents; they are redefining it according to their cultural context. Josh McDowell called this as an attempt to 'put together their own religious canon in a smorgasbord style."[12] The Coconut generation is led to believe that it is better to cut and paste various ideas, beliefs and values in order to construct their own faith. They freely borrow and steal concepts of God, salvation, humanity etc from all religions around them to arrive at one that is right for them. This attitude is popularly called "salad-bar theology" – picking and choosing the view of God that suits us best or can justify my life choices.

Coconuts are also more open-mindedness toward other belief systems. They are immersed in a culture where everything is right and tolerance is the new value. The Coconut generation exemplifies the "question-everything-and-trust-nothing" attitude and are found unsatisfied with half-baked attempts at answering their questions. There is a strong sense of personal entitlement among the youth - "I'm entitled to a good life because I follow God"; Success orientation pervades the minds of Asian Indian immigrants. There is a strong tendency toward individualistic thinking - their commitment to churches and to ministries are determined largely through a self-centered, 'what is in it for me', cost/benefit analysis. The second generation leaders are relational and shy away from hierarchical notions of leadership and the rigid separation of clergy and laity.

The success orientation has fostered a high level of parental pressure on the second generation to attend elite universities, find high paying jobs, and prove to their immigrant parents that their sacrifices have paid off. Some of the second generation ministries are making an intentional attempt to dissuade their members to look beyond the traditional money making career options.

The missional involvement of Indian American churches depends on whether the church is mainline Protestant or evangelical. Most denominational churches are involved with their sister churches back in India. Some of the mainline protestant congregations tend to work on social issues; while the evangelical churches tend towards outreach work or charity efforts even in non-Indian contexts.

Dilemma of Change:
Doing Church the Same Way or Differently?

As time passes, new generations come along, cultures change, and the church is forced to change to be relevant. The tension between the immigrant and Coconut generations has been a chronic problem in many of the Indian churches. The immigrant generation tries to maintain harmony of culturally diverse groups and the Coconut generation feels frustrated as their needs remains unmet.

The Church has always been the same and always changing. We see this in ancient church history, Indian church history, European church history, as well as in American church history. The reformed faith believes in being an ever-reforming faith. The issue of relevancy calls for flexibility of expressions and rigidity on beliefs. Otherwise we loose people as well as beliefs. New waves of changes are

> **IYAD..WYAD...YAG ...WYAG**
> **If You Always Do**
> **What You Always Did**
> **You Always Get**
> **What You Always Got**

breaking on shores of Asian Indian churches in America. The Coconut generation will herald these changes and be catalytic for even more changes in the following generations and Asian Indian Christianity.

"When young people are given lots of independence to do things their way, we find them isolating themselves from the rest of the congregation," said the pastor of growing Indian church in Dallas. "When they are encouraged to participate in church, their parents are unhappy with their music and creative expressions. We are caught between the two generations. The Immigrant generation is unwilling to change or incorporate newer ways of doing church; for them Sunday morning is an important time of the week to be reminiscent about the faith they had grown up with back in India; they don't want to compromise or tweak worship styles in order to make it relevant to their children."

"Who is winning this tug-of-war in your church?" I asked the pastor to gauge which direction it is leaning.

"Of course, in the direction of parents. They are in the governing structures and unwilling to share power with the younger generation. Having built the churches with their hard earned money they want to have it their way most of time. Parents fail to see that they are sacrificing their own children at the altar of their ego and cultural pride."

In 1970, Francis Schaeffer saw the change coming, "The church today should be getting ready and talking about issues of tomorrow and not issues of 20 and 30 years ago, because church is going to be squeezed in a wringer. "[13] The Indian community churches often reminiscence so much about its past that it fails to engage with present or future issues. The "we never did it that way before" syndrome pervades the immigrant generation and a prime cause for resistance to change. Some church leaders are intuitively aware of the problems of the emerging generations, but most are clueless!

Generations often clash on the understanding of immutability and flexibility. Holding on to some things tightly and others loosely, drawing deeply from historic Christian faith and contemporary cultures are marks of Christian leaders in 21st century. No matter how culture changes or Christianity changes, Jesus remain the same "yesterday, today and forever." (Heb 13:8) No matter where the tides take us, we can anchor our souls on Jesus in the turbulent times ahead.

German theologian Jurgen Moltmann accurately located the challenge the church faces in our times as a double crisis – "the crisis of relevancy and crisis of identity. These two crises are complementary. The more theology and church attempt to become relevant to the problems of the present day, the more deeply they are drawn into a crisis of their own identity. The more they attempt to assert their identity in traditional dogmas, rights and moral notions, the more irrelevant and unbelievable they become."[14] Much of the Asian Indian church's identity is closely lined with robes, rituals, liturgies, communication styles, personalities, etc and they feel threatened when the younger generation questions them or attempts to replace them.

The Coconut church will cause the immigrant church to change, not die off. In Christian Ministry some things must never change, while other things must always be changing. The wisdom to know the difference and how we go about it will make all the difference in the future.

Worship Language: English or Indian?

Over the last decade or so, one of the chief complaints of the young people in many Indian churches in America has been "we do not understand anything going on in the church." Their minimal knowledge of Indian languages like Gujurati, Hindi, Malayalam, Tamil, Telugu, etc. kept them from making any sense of the worship services or the sermon. 'I do not get anything from church' is another common complaint. Intangible benefits are often overlooked and immediate needs determine choices they make concerning which church to attend. Some churches tried transliterated liturgies and songs, but that only solved the problem of decoding the worship orders and songs, but not understanding them.

As the young people get older, they are less likely to want to attend an Indian church. Young people are uncomfortable in Indian churches because they cannot understand or speak Indian languages. They simply have no inkling about what is going on. Since language and specific faith traditions are a central piece of the immigrant church culture, the young people feel completely ignored and sidelined.

When a group of young adults made a list of reasons why the church should start an English service, the pastor became angry and shouted at them, "Don't you know this is an Indian church? You all are Indians! You should learn to speak our language."

Young adults felt humiliated by the unsympathetic gesture. Some of them continued to attend church mostly for family obligations and some others started checking local American churches. Tragically a large number of them left the church and dropped out of Christian community all together.

> In worship our relationship with Christ is established, maintained, and repaired. Christ meets us in our act of celebrating his death and resurrection. In this worship encounter, the Spirit brings us the very real benefits of Christ's death - salvation, healing, comfort, hope, guidance, and assurance. Through this encounter, order and meaning come into our lives. Through worship, a right ordering of God, the world, self, and neighbor is experienced, and the worshiper receives a peace that passes understanding. Simply put, worship is an it-is-well-with-my-soul experience.
>
> **Robert Webber**

Then there are churches that started English worship services consisting of few English songs and a translated liturgy or order of worship. Most songs are traditional hymns, taken from the hymnal in the church pews they rented. The immigrant generation is not familiar with these songs or find it hard to relate to. The younger generation viewed the immigrant churches as dysfunctional and hypocritical religious institutions that are modeling a negative expression of Christian spirituality. Secondly, there were continual clashes between the generations over issues involving cultural differences in the styles and philosophies of church leadership as well as control.

The choir was replaced with praise and worship teams and organ gave in to electronic keyboards and drums. The hymnbooks disappeared, and the words to the praise music were flashed on the screens. Modern dramas were added and announcements were no longer spoken, but only given via large screens and bulletins.

Worship must transcend the limits of language, yet our linguistic skills play an important role. Some of the non-Christian families are more intentional in teaching their mother tongues to their young. The cultural associations like Tamil Sangham, Gujurati Samaj, Malayalee Association, etc. are more intentional on language education. Some of them provide classes on Indian classical music, instruments and dances. Some Tamil churches run regular classes on Tamil for their young.

Teaching Indian languages has become a major thrust in many Indian churches. "If they learn Malayalam," a visiting Syrian church clergy told me recently as I dropped him to the airport, "all the issues with the second generation can be addressed well. It is only our kids who have not shown any inclination to learning their mother tongues. Nor have our parents had the time or commitment to teach." Things are not as simple as that. Although language proficiency is an important indicator, the wider concept of culture holds the key to generational cleavage.

Different Notions of Church:

The conflicts between the Indian Christian immigrants and their American born children arise out of three fundamental cleavages – the intergenerational gap, a fundamental difference in worldview and different models of Christianity.[15] The first two we have covered in earlier chapters and the third cleavage exists as the immigrant generation is part of a traditional denominational church and their children are more inclined to post-denominational independent churches or para-churches ministries, both of which also tries to impose their version of Christianity on the other.

The first generation views the church primarily as a place where their offspring will be taught morals, experience ethnic community and preserve the faith of their forefathers. They collectively uphold certain cultural idiosyncrasies and values and attempt to enforce them on the budding generation. Some churches take up the argument of the unchanging traditions and need for its continuation for the sake of itself. They believe that the traditions that have stood the test of time, which have served their community well through many generations, will serve the emerging generation of Indians in America as well.

> Our experiences from the past are to give us the confidence to face the challenges of tomorrow. We are not to build monuments but to join the movement. Sometimes we choose instead to build monastries. .... When the church becomes a movement and not a monastery she becomes a place of transformation for the very culture from which we run in fear.
>
> Erwin McManus

The Coconut generation leaders reject sharp distinctions between clergy and laity and have made conscious efforts to blur the lines within their churches. In immigrant churches, respect and honor are oftentimes given automatically to the pastors just by virtue of their title. However, for the second generation, titles do not necessarily ensure respect. They embrace the notion of the priesthood of all believers and believe that all need to serve the body of Christ in practical ways by exercising their spiritual gifts. They place a high priority on its members discovering, developing, and deploying their spiritual gifts. They stress all followers of Christ to be ministers and the distinction between professional minister and laity as a man-made distinction. They are informed by the study of the Reformation, global missionary efforts, teachings, and the life examples of many influential Christian leaders in America.

For thousands of years Indian society has been organized socially according to the caste system and the social function determined their status in the society in a hierarchical manner. Even Christian priests by default came to be seen as Brahmins. The first generation gave the due respect for priests according to Indian traditions, but the second generation saw things differently; they saw their pastor as a friend and an equal before God. A young Coconut was strongly chastised by his parents and pastor when he returned from college and called his pastor by his first name. "We are all equal in Christ and there was no place for hierarchical thinking," he said.

This is true of Korean and Chinese community churches too. The second and third generations did not bow before their pastors and this was taken as a serious offence by the first generation folks. For many pastors and church leaders, loyalty to the pastor and faithfulness to the ministry of the church are one and the same thing. This is certainly not so with the second generation. They have divided between the two and for many Christ followers the later takes precedence over the former.

The issue of change and relevancy is deeply contested and exposes the differing view of both generations. While talking to an Indian Orthodox priest, this issue came up. "Do you think, we need to change to keep up with the times?" I asked him.

"Do we change, simply for the sake of it? How sure can one be that whatever change we make is going to work?"

"Why rock the boat? Our faith has kept us through more changing times than the emerging generation of immigrants in America. Remember, our faith is two thousand years old. It has withstood foreign invasion, Catholicization, colonialism, modernity, communism and what not."

"But many of our younger generation do not know those stories of history of Christianity in India." I interrupted him.

"That is precisely the point. The first generation bears the responsibility of sharing it with their children. But unfortunately, they also do not know this either. They have a superficial notion of church doctrines, practices and history of Christianity. Neither do they understand the meaning of our faith traditions nor have they experienced any genuine transformation in their own lives. They simply are going through motions every Sunday. I won't blame them either. The immigrant generation sacrificed much by coming to a new land and trying to establish and provide for their families. And in all those pursuits, seeking a deeper understanding of their faith and taking time to relate to their children were left out."

"Okay. Look at other Orthodox churches like Greek or Russian. We find mass exodus of younger generations and yet it prevailed through many decades. So do you think the Indian Orthodox Churches will be around and what places does it have in the Western Christendom?"

> The bend of the road is not the end of the road unless you fail to make the curve.
> Anonymous

"Yea, our young people are dropping out. But many western young people are getting interested in Orthodox rituals and eastern practices. They call them postmodern youths, I think."

Nobody knows what is going to happen in the future, but one thing is sure – this generation is rocking the boat and has forced us to think about questions that we are not comfortable with. Only time will tell what shape Indian American churches will take, but surely they are going to be different from what it is now.

The American way of dealing with church issues are more direct, analytical and objective. When a problem arises in a congregation, they do a systematic study of the situation, explore all possible solutions to the problem and draw out cost-benefit matrix. They present feasible solutions in a proposal to the board and carefully study the proposal objectively and explore viable options and back it with their personal commitment, good will and funds. It is more like seeking a solution for a scientific problem and much like problem solving in the American corporate world. The American born generation expects church issues to be dealt with in a similar manner.

On the contrary, the Indian way of solving problems is very different. First, we will try to think there is no problem. Then we will try to put up a brave front and cover up all signs of the problem. But those who are at the front lines or receiving end of the problem know the consequence of the problem. If at all they admit the problem and want to find some solutions, they want to do it without offending anyone. They try to please everyone, maintain status quo, and group preservation takes priority. Keeping unhealthy groups together takes precedence over treating the sickness. Eventually what happens is that churches become filled with sick people, literally. Then comes the major hurdle of 'we have always done things in this way.' Elders and pastors are often overwhelmed by the needs of the community that they do not want to take up new issues. Not to mention the overall resistance to any change, even change for the better of the community. The Indian way of inter-relationship networks keeps from objective evaluation from a theoretical foundation. Questions concerning issues become "Is this the *best* way to do it?" instead of "Is this the *right* thing to do?"

To make matters worse, people have their own cliques in the congregation and are able to divide it to serve individual egos. Character assassination, put downs, and politicking are all too common. When our young people see how their parents are handling issues and treating other Christian adults, they get disillusioned. Sometimes very unchristian behaviors are displayed even by our leaders. "Why should I be part of such a mean set of people? I really saw their true colors at the last general body meeting." I am not saying one approach is better than the other, but that there are fundamental differences in how we handle conflicts. It would be difficult to keep everyone together for a long time where there is such deep-seated disparity.

Church Drop Outs: Why Aren't the Youth Coming to Church Anymore?

"Nobody understands me!" – A common lament of young people in Indian churches which are generally shrugged off by most adults and pastors. What these young people are really asking is, "Is there anyone out there who cares?" Somehow this generation seems to have given up on all organized religions, including Christianity. The Coconut generation does not have the same levels of emotional ties to Asian heritage as their parents do and immigrant churches do not meet their needs or expectations as it does for their parents.

Top 10 reasons why Coconut Generation is dropping out of the Immigrant churches

1. I do not get anything out of it.
2. Church is a club
3. Church is full of hypocrites
4. More interested in my money than me
5. Politics in Church
6. Lack of engaging and relevant music/ sermons
7. Lack of authenticity
8. Dull and Boring
9. Unfriendly to visitors and small children
10. Other good alternatives churches

The denominational identification and loyalty is waning quickly with the Coconut generation. As they come-of-age and stand on their own feet, they are increasingly inclined to think that church association is a matter of their own choice. This is evident from decreasing involvement, participation and giving. Just because they grew up in a particular church setting, does not mean they need to go there all their life. This generation who changes jobs, cars and even homes like clothes, find it strange to commit to a church all their life. Yet at the same time, they want a community that they can grow old with, who is in the same socio-cultural-economic class as they are and have similar spiritual goals. The Church needs to win the loyalty of every generation and the Coconut generation cannot be taken for granted.

As many youths in their late teen and 20s are turning away from the faith of their families, college ministries are becoming a crucial element in reaching this generation. Both churched and unchurched Coconuts are open to 'checking out' spiritual realities while in college. No wonder the college years are the time when Christ makes His deepest mark and changes the course of many Coconuts. In the neutral setting of a college campus, Christ's claims are seen and heard with new eyes and ears. The faithful college based ministries provide ample avenue for them not only to embrace the truth, but also help them cultivate a vibrant relationship with Jesus Christ. At the same time, Coconuts are bombarded with Hindu rituals, Buddhist ideals and new-age philosophy and they check them out with equal curiosity. The main religious groups on campuses are evangelical Christians, Muslims and increasingly, Hindus. The campus ministry organizations have shown remarkable effectiveness in reaching this generation and I believe the church and campus ministries need to work together, as they have much to offer to each other. Some non-evangelical traditional Indian church leaders also feel threatened by Christian ministries in college campuses and ask their children not to associate with them.

But this is not an Indian American Church phenomenon only. In spite of many contemporary approaches, many churches feel they are loosing ground with the younger generation. Young people are staying away from churches and appear to be exploring other faiths and spiritual beliefs. The statistical researcher George Barna observed that young people in their late teens and twenties are the least likely to attend church in a typical week.[16] Once, a Hindu priest in New Jersey told me that their young people are not coming to temple like their parents. There is something about being young these days and their quest for spiritual matters that organized religion is not attractive to them anymore.

The Coconut generation tends to think, "Is it wrong to expect some kind of perfection from the church? Should a church be a replica of the world? Should I settle for a god who is less than perfect? I want church to draw me to God and help me to focus on God, which I sometimes am not able to do through the daily grind of life. I want to experience God's presence and power in my life. I would like to hear inspiring sermons with real-life applications. I want to be part of a genuine spiritual community, not just a cultural one. Help me become a better person and to be part of the eternal drama of God. Is that too much to ask? Should I continue to be part of a church, which means nothing to me? Why should I continue to be part of my parents' church? Isn't the faith community that I belong to a matter of my personal choice?"

I asked a young lady in the parking lot of an Indian church, "Why do you come to this church?" Her answer was typical for many Coconuts. "Primarily because of family obligations and then for social reasons. I cannot make any sense of it all. It does not help me a bit. I am out of that loop completely. I see church more like a club, a bunch of people come there to play politics and meet their socio-cultural needs. It has nothing to do with spirituality or

God. It is all a boring stuff, especially the preaching!"

That was more than I asked for and I wanted to probe her mind further. So I asked her, "If you don't mind, tell me about today's sermon? What was helpful? What was boring?"

The answer was quick and frank, "Everything was dull. Nothing got my attention. The pastor does not relate to real life, or have any clue of what really is going on in the lives of his listeners. The Indian accent is very annoying. He tries to hide it, but it keeps coming up again and again."

Even as some drop out of Indian churches completely, many others choose the balancing act of shuttling between parent's church and a local American church.

"Is anything wrong with being part of two or more churches at the same time?" asked Cindy a resident of northern suburb of Chicago. She continued, "Like I go to the Indian church to experience community and an American Bible church for worship and teaching." I know many in the ethnic second generation churches who are faced with this dilemma every week. To prod her thinking further, I asked her, "Why do you go to two churches? Is your loyalty divided?"

> Let no Christian parents fall into the delusion that Sunday School is intended to ease them of their personal duties. The first and most natural condition of things is for Christian parents to train up their own children in the nurture and admonition of the Lord.
> **Charles Haddon Spurgeon**

She replied promptly, "The lack of Biblical teaching in the Indian Church, I supplement by going to a good Bible teaching church. I need that for my spiritual growth. We can never get every nutrient from the food we eat; food supplements are part of regular diet these days, right?"

In order to glean her insights on this issue I asked her, "Cindy, what about your membership?" as she was thinking I kept shooting follow up questions, "Where would you call home? Where do you belong to? Where will you get married? Where would you like to raise your children? Who will bury you, when you die?" I stopped with that one as I felt that I am asking her too many questions. I did not want to intimidate her and only wanted to take a peek into her mind on this complex matter.

But she answered decisively, "I have thought a lot about it. You see, I was born and baptized in the Indian church. I went there all my life until I went away to college in Urbana Champaign. I came to a personal relationship with Jesus Christ outside of the church in a campus fellowship. Now I am back here in Chicago for work and I attend two churches regularly. I haven't taken membership anywhere yet. But since my parents still belong to this church, I guess, I am still a member there. But I give my tithes to the American church, because I believe in what they do and they benefit me a lot in my spiritual walk. I come to the Indian church to experience the Indian community, to meet with childhood friends and also to serve in whatever capacity I could. I feel obliged to help my younger brothers and sisters to know Christ personally or encourage them in their walk with the Lord."

"But when it comes to marriage," she continued, "I would like it to be in the Indian service. You see marriage involves more than me. It is a family affair and our entire community will be involved. Also if I get married in a court or other church, it would make my parents very unhappy. But I do not mind getting married to non-Indians."

I am amazed at how adeptly this generation rejects and holds on to Indian and American customs simultaneously. This is their strength, emanating from the way they are wired uniquely from within. Duality of the identity and having learned to balance between the brownness and whiteness gets reflected in matters of faith issues as well. They have learned to take advantage of their uniqueness. They are comfortable switching between the two worlds so seamlessly and effortlessly, helping them to make most of all that is available to them. Although their commitment to God is exclusive, their church participation is not.

Coconut Ministry: Six Emerging Models

In spite of the many challenges the Americanized Asian Indian generation and the immigrant Indian church faces, there are many traces of effective models of ministry among them. Coconut generation is responding to the love of Christ seen at Calvary and are bringing an unique sense of passion in reaching their generation for Christ.

Before we explore the specific models of Coconut ministry, Kenda Dean's insight on the quest of the young for passion and doing passionate ministry would be helpful. She writes in her book, *Practicing Passion: Youth and Quest for a Passionate Church,* that adolescence is characterized by passion and that ministry with youth needs to be predicated on passion - the passion of Christ, the passion of youth and the passionate faith that results when these two come together. In a consumer culture, which seems to focus on self-fulfillment the passion of Christ subversively calls us to self -giving love. Kenda suggests that enabling youth to live passionately in the life, death and resurrection of Christ is precisely what they are longing and looking for. But often the church is passionless or afraid of passion - discipleship is so easily about socializing young people into our (adult) way of behaving and being sensible, nice and respectable rather than unleashing their passion into being dangerous followers and lovers of Christ. She suggests that the way to do so is to develop a curriculum of passion - introducing young people to the ancient practices of the Christian faith which are transformative. These practices are ultimately about enabling a community to be imitators of Christ transformed into his likeness. Without such focus youth ministry loses its purpose and ends up being about entertainment and cool youth leaders.

There has been many concerted efforts to effectively minister to the Coconut generation in a culturally relevant manner, most of which falls into one of the following six categories.

1. **Church-based Youth Ministry:** Most of the Indian churches in America have at least a lay-led youth fellowship. Youth groups will mature to the next stage with formally or informally trained leaders arising from among them. Churches are beginning to employ professional youth workers and provide greater support for youth ministry within the church. Some try to integrate youths into congregational life and see them as full partners in every aspect of the faith community.

2. **Church within a Church:** Some of the immigrant churches have recognized the generational differences and have permitted youths to function as an independent church doing culturally relevant ministry. The Coconut leaders enjoy greater autonomy and support of their parents, yet stick to the broad doctrinal beliefs of the parent church. Most of the worship services will be in English with their unique style and approach to ministry. This approach prepares youth group to become a new church; youth pastor becomes the pastor of the new congregation; new church is formed with a blessing of the mother church; it comes with its share of operational conflicts like two generations under one roof.

3. "Amorphous" Ministry: Many Coconuts work outside the walls of existing churches and concentrate on incarnational and relational ministry through local bible study, home fellowships, coffeehouses, music, sports and other non-church expressions. They are more like an affinity group and less like church. The informality is a big attraction for those who are disillusioned with institutional religious structures and cultural churches. It leverages peer level influence and accountability and handles generational issues more effectively.

4. College Campus Ministry: The battlefield for this generation has shifted to college campuses. The presence of Asian Indians in American universities is at record-breaking levels. Without the overarching religious overtones of the parents and ethnic community or culture, they are trying to carve their own unique identity and explore spirituality more freely. In the last couple of years, Indian Americans have appeared on the radars of most campus and student ministry organizations and they have assigned personnel and resources to minister to Asian Indians on campuses.

5. New Church Plant: Some young leaders from the Coconut generation have ventured out with a core team to plant new churches for their generation. They enjoy the most freedom to create their own philosophy of ministry, staffing and styles of worship and teaching. They target people who have dropped out of traditional Indian churches and others from their own generation. In the last few years, many young people from this generation have sensed God's call to ministry and enrolled in seminaries with a prime objective of preparing themselves to plant new churches for their generation.

6. India Focus Groups in American Congregations: An increasing number of American churches have become aware of the "browning" of their neighborhood with Indians and have begun to reach out and include them. Many of these churches have ethnic centered focus groups that meet after Sunday service or during the week with their own programs and budget. Many from the Coconut generation and late immigrants who could not fit into churches planted by earlier immigrants find this very attractive.

To Ponder About:

1. What is your church experience? How has it helped or impeded your faith walk?

2. What has changed and what remains same in your church? Why?

3. How is Coconut generation's faith and spirituality different from the immigrant generation?

4. Try to recollect names of kids who went to Sunday school with you. Where are they now in the faith journey? What helped them to stick with church and what caused some to drop out?

5. Where do you find yourself among the six emerging models? What makes you feel connected there? Why?

Endnotes

[1] Raymond William, *Religions of Immigrants from India and Pakistan: New Threads in the American Tapestry*, (Cambridge: Cambridge University Press, 1988).

[2] Ronald Takaki, *Strangers from a Different Shore: A History of Asian Americans*, (New York: Penguin Books, 1989) 295.

[3] Tony Carnes and Fenggang Yang eds., *Asian American Religion*, (New York: New York University Press, 2004), 30.

[4] Based on a report by The Council of Hindu Temples in North America – www. councilofhindutemples.org (accessed May 10, 2005).

[5] I am yet to see any broad based research done in this area. Even some of the associations and federations representing Indian Christians in America could not furnish any data in this regard. The fluid nature of many small or home churches and large scale division along the lines of language, denomination, doctrines etc. makes it difficult to assess this accurately.

[6] For the history of Indian churches in America, see Raymond Williams, *Religious Immigrants from Indian and Pakistan: New Threads in the American Tapestry*, *(Cambridge: Cambridge University Press, 1988),* T.M. Thomas, *Kerala Immigrants in America,* (Cochin: Simons Printers, 1984) and Thomas Idiculla ed. S*trangers in a Foreign Land: Indian Pentecostal Community in the United States*, (Boston: Cummings & Hathaway Publishers, 1998).

[7] Michael Emerson and Christian Smith, *Divided by Faith, (*Oxford: Oxford University Press, 2000).

[8] Ibid. 116.

[9] For more on this, see Darrell Guder's book *Missional Church: A Vision for the Sending of the Church*, (Grand Rapids: Eerdmans, 1998).

[10] A good place to engage in this conversation is the book by the Catholic missionary to Africa Vincent Donovan, *Rediscovering Christianity* (Maryknoll, NY: Orbis, 1987).

[11] Kenda Dean, *Practicing Passion: Youth and the Quest for a Passionate Church* (Grand Rapids: Eerdmans, 2004).

[12] Josh McDowell, *Beyond Belief to Conviction*, (Wheaton: Tyndale House, 2003), 10.

[13] Francis Schaeffer, *The Church at the End of the 20th Century*, (Chicago: IV Press, 1970), 81-82.

[14] Jurgen Moltmann, *The Crucified God* (New York: Harper & Row, 1974) 7.

[15] Prema Kurien, Christian by Birth or Rebirth? Generation and Difference in an Indian American Christian Church in *Asian American Religion*, 161. Also see Donald Miller's *Reinventing American Protestantism: Christianity in the New Millennium,* (Berkeley: University of California Press, 1997).

[16] George Barna, Church Attendance Report – 2004. See http://www.barna.org/FlexPage.aspx?Page=Topic&TopicID=10 (Accessed May 10, 2005)

8

Same Boat:
Lessons for Ministry to Coconuts

Learning without thought is labor lost;
thought without learning is perilous.
– *Confucius (551 BC - 479 BC)*

Asian Indians in America have much in common with the rest of the Asians in America and there are many lessons to learn from them. A story comes to mind from the writing of Amy Tan, a popular Chinese American author. In her novel *The Joy Luck Club,* she describes a mother-daughter conflict:

> "You want me to be someone I'm not!" I sobbed. "I'll never be the kind of daughter you want me to be!"

> "Only two kinds of daughters," she shouted in Chinese. "Those who are obedient and those who follow their own mind! Only one kind of daughter can live in this house. Obedient daughter!"

> "Then I wish I wasn't your daughter. I wish you weren't my mother," I shouted back.

Conflicts between mother and teenage daughter are common to all cultures, but scenarios like this play out in Indian American homes almost everyday.

In this chapter, I hope to explore other Asian Americans and their struggle with the second generation and how church and ministries are dealing with them. It is intended to help us learn from other Asian experiences so that we can effectively translate these lessons into our communities and churches and to avoid some of the mistakes they have made. This is too ambitious even to attempt and might seem to generalize on many Asian cultures and churches. So please bear with me as I tread into this vast minefield. I am compelled to include this as I have learned much from other Asian cultures and wonderful Christian leaders that I have come across over the years.

The generational difference and similarity between various Asian American communities came to me rather unexpectedly in seminary during an intensive course on 'Asian American Counseling'. I signed up for a class thinking it might remotely help me understand issues of care ministry among the Korean American churches. But I was pleasantly surprised at the introductory class when I met a fourth generation Japanese American, a third generation Chinese American, a Singaporean, a second generation Filipino American, many Korean Americans from various generations and another Indian American. I was amazed that the issues of the emerging generation in all these communities had many common threads. This class also helped me gain deeper appreciation of many of the East Asian cultures that I had closely interacted with during my days in the corporate world and the Asian American pastors and churches that I had come to know during my time in California. One comment that stood out in my mind from that class was after one intense discussion on generations across cultures, one of my classmates concluded, "We all are in the same boat." And that is how I got the title of this chapter.

Diaspora Ministry: Scattered

As Asian Indians, we have the benefit of learning from other Asians who have migrated to the Untied States before us. The challenges that we face with the younger generation are not anything new; other communities and churches have faced them before us and many others are facing it right now. There is so much to observe, interact, dialogue and learn from each other, if only we are open to learning.

Although much of the Asian Indian immigration to America is a late twentieth century phenomena, other Asians were here earlier. In spite of the fact that Indian cultures are distinct in many ways as compared to East Asian countries, there are amazing similarities between them. Some common features among many immigrants, particularly Asians, is the strong family system, traditional values, and kinship culture. They exhibit the strong tendency to make sacrifices for their sake of the children; not to mention strong emphasis on education and work ethics common among the first generation. Hard work, frugality, strong interpersonal affinity and group solidarity are characteristics of people from the region. Their emerging generations battled with issues of ethnic identity and assimilation in many of the same ways that Indians do.

> **Those who had been scattered, preached the word wherever they went.**
> **Acts 8:4**

Within Chinese, Japanese and Korean immigrant churches, males with official church positions, professional status, Bible knowledge, and age tend to hold power. They exercise power informally through relationships of obligation and face-saving norms.[1] Much of it is true in Indian American churches with the additional parameter of caste. Koreans may have a more individualistic outlook than the group-oriented Chinese, Japanese and Indians. The second generation questions the values and lifestyles of their parents in most Asian American settings. The new generation reflects the growing openness of American society, even as Asian family and community offer more supportive framework for their younger generation than mainstream American society.

In most East Asian American churches you will find the influence of Confucian thought. It establishes hierarchical (based on age, gender or position) order within the society with submission as mandatory moral obligation for achieving cosmic harmony. The notion of authority and respect has moral legitimacy between ruler and ruled, elder and youth, husband and wife etc. This is much akin to Indian churches which shows significant influence of Hindu ideologies. Caste-based thinking, inferiority of women, respect of the elders, oppressive power structures etc. can be found across denominations in Indian American churches also.

Like the emerging generation of East Asian Americans, the Coconuts are less eager to resolve contradictions in a variety of situations. The ability to perform amidst blatant contradictions is their strength. They are quick to jump to conclusions and to write off the immigrant spirituality and church rituals, without making any effort to understand why they do what they do.

To some extent the generational experiences and ministry principles are translatable. The experiences of the second generation of Indian Americans are much like the second generation of Chinese American and Korean Americans. Just like in Indian American churches, Asian Americans attend churches to advance their career, project status, wealth, show-off their dress, car, or brag about their children's educational attainment. The immigrant generation's ambitious outlook on life and insatiable appetite for wealth and status make churches a perfect platform to press forward their own agenda rather than to gather together to worship, serve or discover their greater purposes in life. This not only causes the second generation to see their parent's generation as hypocritical, but to be cynical about church, spirituality and God. A generation who wants to be 'free to be who they are' feels frustrated and disenchanted.

Moreover, continuing research and literature from the Asian American community can be borrowed meaningfully for emerging generations of the Indian community. In light of these and other reasons, I strongly believe that the Coconut generation leaders and the Indian American church must interface with other Asian American churches and ministries for insights on growing effective ministry with appropriate contextualization. I will limit the discussion in this chapter to Chinese, Japanese and Koreans for lack of space.

Chinese Americans:

The Chinese have a much longer history in America than Indians, and the Chinese presence can be observed from the Californian Gold rush in 1849. Chinatowns, Chinese food, martial arts, Chinese New Year celebrations, Chinese businesses, etc. play a dominant role in the entire Chinese community and have become regular features of the American landscape. The First Chinese

> Tell me and I will forget,
> Show me and I may not remember.
> Involve me, and I will understand.
> - Chinese Proverb

church was started in 1853 in San Francisco as the mission of an American denomination[2], unlike the transplanted model of Indian Christianity in America. By 1995, there were over 700 Chinese churches in America and most of them did not have any affiliation with American denominations.[3]

The first generation Chinese immigrants of the post-1965

immigration have vivid memories of communist persecution of Christians and the Cultural Revolution of the 70's and have significantly shaped the religious dynamics of Chinese American churches. The three broad categories of Chinese are OBC (Overseas-born Chinese), ABC (American-born Chinese) and ARC (American-raised Chinese). OBCs are born overseas in places like Hong Kong, Taiwan, Singapore, etc. and have now come to settle in America. Many Chinese churches have separate services for OBC and ABC/ARCs in order to effectively cater to their different needs. Earlier service is conducted in Mandarin or Cantonese and people are formally dressed, while later service is completely in English and informal in every way.

The Chinese Christians who are influenced by Confucianism want their American-born or raised children to follow cherished traditional moral values and virtues. However, Americanized young people do not easily accept tradition or parents as sources of authority. In the Chinese community the younger generation does not buy into parental remarks "do this because we have done this for generations" or 'do this because I (parent) am saying so". Sounds a lot like the Indian community, right? Yet some youth leaders and pastors have found the authority of God as a good substitute for the preservation of Confucian moral values.

A Chinese counselor friend once told me, "Biblical values are more consistent with Asian values. Respect for older people, obedience to parents, lifelong marriages etc., are the bedrock foundations of the Asian society. We must help American-born kids to see how Bible is more consistent with Asian culture than American."

I asked him, "But won't this create inner conflict as they see themselves as American and their parents are pressing them to become more Chinese? Won't it be wrong to use Scripture to 'manipulate' their allegiance to Asian ways?"

"Not at all," my friend responded immediately, "We only have to show it to them. They have to make the choice between two sets of values. They have to evaluate the consequences and make a set of values to guide their life through. I have grown to healthy appreciation of my Chinese roots now, although once I hated everything Chinese for the way it was shown to me. We should refrain from twisting their arms to obedience or decide on their behalf, but allow them to choose for themselves."

A Chinese pastor talking of the identity struggles of American-born Chinese young people said,

"On the one hand, every human being is a unique person. On the other hand, a person bears the identity of gender, race, family, ethnicity, nationality, religious faith and so on. The issue of identity becomes a problem when we place value on the identities that one holds. Some identities are better than others. We find it hard to obtain 'superior identity' and reject our 'inferior identity.' Scripture tell us that God creates all human beings in his own image. Jesus Christ came to redeem human being from sin and restore their fallen image to his likeness. All men and women, Jews or Gentiles, the free or slave are therefore equally invaluable in the eyes of Jesus Christ. It is mandatory for all Christians holding multiple identities to live out the gospel message of Jesus Christ."[4]

The concept of "adhesive identities" is a helpful way to understand the dilemma of multiple identities that the Coconut generation struggles with as well. Instead of either assimilating by abandoning ethnicity or simply preserving ethnicity in sacrifice of assimilation, this concept of adhesive identity opens the possibility of holding both American and ethnic identities simultaneously. Ethnic Americans are at the forefront of multiple identity and identity integration issues and the emerging Indian Americans have much to learn from them and also contribute to them.

According to Fennang Yang, the Chinese Protestant churches in America tend to be conservative in theology. Many Chinese Christians are evangelical and some are influenced by American fundamentalism, which clearly manifests itself by restraining women from leadership roles.[5] He also claimed that "Chinese Christian church has become the institutional base for passing on transformed Confucian values to younger generation."[6] This leads me to ask the question: Where do Indian churches in America stand in its theology and what values will she pass on to the next generation? And is there any relationship between those observations to the Chinese Church?

Also, a lesson worth noting is that ethnic Christianity is not going to close down with the emergence of another generation. In spite of difference in language, modernization, socio-economic life, etc. Chinese churches have grown and thrived with every generation. Ethnicity or national origin is one of the main sources for denominationalism in the United States.[7] And the immigrant churches have played a crucial role in identity construction of its emerging generations and vice versa, while both flourish in meeting the needs of their respective constituencies.

Japanese Americans:

The first Japanese Christian group was formed by eight students in 1877 in San Francisco[8]. Japanese churches were established by the immigrants to meet the need for companionship and mutual support while living in a hostile and alien society. They served as cultural havens. They celebrated Japanese holidays in churches. In many Indian immigrant churches too, sometimes the distinction between religious and cultural celebration cannot be demarcated.

The Japanese immigrants have used some forms of the numeric to distinguish between generations. The first generation are called "issei" (ichi = one), the second generation is "nisei"; the third generation, "sansei"; the fourth, "yonsei" and the fifth, "gosei". The Nisei who were sent to Japan for education were called "kibei". Will the Indian American community be able to track generationally? Is that necessary or does that matter?

From the third generation Japanese American era, beginning in the 1970's, we can learn that generational references will begin to lose meaning and there will be greater mixing up of generations. The common culture and symbols will come to define the community beyond the third generation.

Also, fourth and fifth generations are the most "American" of any Japanese groups. The new American values appear more comfortable for each new generation. Many families and churches include as many as four generations.

The Japanese Americans have maintained less interaction with other Asian American communities, because of the strong anti-Japanese feelings among Asian immigrants who experienced Japanese colonization. The Japanese churches began as exclusively ethnic, and worship services were conducted mostly in Japanese in all Issei congregations. English services were introduced as the American-born generation began to take part. Churches remained ethnic but served both Japanese and English-speaking groups. The Nisei generation created most of the religious organizations for Japanese Americans during the 1920's-40's and most are still active.[9]

After many generations and a high rate of intermarriages, the churches have become pan-Asian churches (mostly East Asians). Among all Asians, the Japanese show the highest rate of intermarriages (over 50% for many years) and is sign that some of the previous stigma about Japanese and dominant groups have diminished[10]. A Japanese American pastor in San Francisco once advised me, "As interracial marriages become more common around the world, I hope our churches will learn to accept, embrace, love and share with these dear brothers and sisters. Let us shed our Asian prejudices and truly practice unity that the Spirit of Christ can bring about. Also let us celebrate our uniqueness and our collective richness of cultures."

Korean Americans:

A popular saying among Korean American churchgoers is: "When the Chinese came to America, they started restaurants; when the Japanese came to America, they started business corporations; when Koreans came to America, they started churches!" I do not know what could be said of Indians in America! Korean churches are one of the fastest growing ethnic churches in America[11]. You can find a Korean church for almost every denomination, generation and ministry philosophy.

The Korean presence in America began in 1903 with the immigration to Hawaii as a result of the Korea-America Treaty of 1882. Subsequent to the Korean War in 1945, immigration to America grew rapidly and the third wave of migration came in 1965 with changes in immigration laws. The Korean American church history also coincides with their immigration – first, one Hawaii Korean Methodist church in 1903, and another one in Los Angels Korean Presbyterian Church in 1905.[12]

Confucianism is generally considered the main ideology governing Korean society, but Buddhism and early missionary efforts of Christian mission agencies made significant impacts on them.

The Korean churches have played an important role in their community life in America. It was the socio-cultural nerve center of the community as it met many needs of the immigrants – practice religious rituals, ethnic identity, source of moral values, and a resource for newly arriving immigrants. It has served as a place to meet with others like themselves and to keep in touch with their culture, like the use of native dress, language, food etc., much like the Indian community in America. The Church serves as a place for ethnic identification and celebration of culture more than spiritual nurture, which turns out to be offensive to the emerging generation as they cannot fully appreciate emphasis on certain peculiarities. The attempts at religious socialization annoys the emerging generation and are often seen as cultural imperialism.

One big lesson for me personally has been the Koreans' dependence on prayer. They believe in the power of prayer and pray passionately and with urgency. The Korean Christians brought with them their tradition of praying consistently and with great faith that the Lord hears and has promised to answer. Many Korean immigrants have been part of the revival that swept through South Korea in late 20th century and the prayer has profoundly shaped their churches and people.

Another major lesson from Korean American churches is their vision for missions. The mission bug has bitten Korean Christians and they have become the second largest mission sending force in the world after Americans. The Korean Americans have a due share in the global mission enterprise. I personally have met Korean American missionaries in many different parts of the world, from Latin America to Africa to Central Asia, the Middle East, and even in India. Indian American churches have a great deal to learn from the Korean American church movement in sending missionaries to the ends of the earth.

Church dropouts are as much a concern in Korean American

churches as in Indian churches in America. Helen Lee called it the "silent exit" of the second generation from churches.[13] The widespread discontentment and inability to keep diverse groups together were a fertile ground to start new churches, which young Korean Americans with seminary education and pioneering spirit exploited to the fullest. But unlike Indian Christians who came from backgrounds as variant as Orthodox, Catholic, Reformed, Protestant, Evangelical and Pentecostal, most Korean Americans came from Protestant Christian backgrounds and their theological differences were minimal.

The 'conversion' of many of the Coconut generation to evangelical Christianity in college campuses or to other neighborhood churches that they regularly plug in, result in intergenerational conflicts just as in Korean and Chinese American students. When they first drop out of ethnic Indian denominational churches, they tend to check out non-ethnic para-churches or non-denominational churches. Some of them experienced racism and exclusion in those groups and returned to ethnic churches or completely dropped out of religious circles altogether. Those who returned fought to obtain greater autonomy in their denominational churches or were forced to form independent ethnic churches, mostly following the lines of American evangelical churches. This trend is beginning to play out in the Indian American community, and similar tendencies can be found among the Korean American second generation.[14]

The language dilemma can be seen in Korean churches too. Many Korean congregations have taken a dual approach - English-speaking services targeted at the younger generation and Korean-speaking services for immigrants. But the younger generation still feel marginalized as they fail to fit into the larger community. Korean churches in America are not effectively meeting the spiritual and social needs of their young people.[15] The generational tension is more pronounced in many Korean American churches than other Asian American congregations and we can learn from and omit many of its mistakes.

On many university campuses, Koreans have maintained two Korean fellowships – one comprised of immigrant students and another comprise of second or third generation Korean students. The first group often complains that American-born Korean students do not know how to speak Korean and are not polite to older Koreans; while the second group complain that immigrant students are too authoritarian, too conservative and that they discriminate against female students. A close parallel can be drawn with Indian American students in some campuses.

The Korean Americans have also brought gender issues in church to the surface. Traditional Asian churches in America are seen as patriarchal institutions and much like the Indian churches, visible gender discrepancies can be seen in many of the Korean churches. Feminization of church attendance, large numbers of women pursuing theological education (compared to other Asians), greater egalitarian spirit of emerging Korean Americans, etc. have given rise to women demanding more ministry opportunities for themselves. While some scholars illustrate the "silencing of women's experience and marginalization of women"[16] in Korean churches, others have welcomed women to be a "bridge maker and cross-bearer"[17] in the context of Korean American churches. Although Indian immigrant women have pursued professional careers, at church they settle for traditional gender-specific subservient roles. The Korean American church may have something to tell us about the growing struggles of women in the church and their expanding ministry roles.

Generational Issues:
What Can Coconut Leaders Learn?

Several second generation Asian American churches are highly influenced by the seeker-sensitive models popularized by rapidly growing evangelical mega-churches such as Willow Creek Community Church in Chicago and Saddleback Community Church in Southern California. The younger Asian Americans, who attend Christian campus fellowships that are primarily evangelical, tend to gravitate towards theologically like-minded congregations. One of the central tenets of their highly evangelistic and seeker-sensitive model is that churches should create an environment within their worship services that are attractive, non-threatening, and non-alienating for non-Christians.

Although worship styles and administrative structures may resemble mainstream, seeker-sensitive, or "new paradigm churches," second generation churches are not mirror copies of mainstream churches. In fashioning their own unique expressions of spirituality, the younger ministers feel that there are several elements of immigrant spirituality that need to be preserved and practiced within their newly formed churches. Most importantly, many believe that immigrants better understand and practice the key Biblical concept of community because they come from a Confucian society that stresses the importance of the collective over the individual. Rejecting the American cultural paradigm of individualism and the ways in which that paradigm has shaped American Christianity, second generation churches aim to embrace the centrality of community.

Some of the Chinese, Korean and Japanese churches have evolved into pan-Asian congregations. It is an expression of rejection of the hierarchy and authoritarian structure of particular ethnic groups in order to embrace a broader group of ethnicities, even as they remain ambivalent to the full-fledged multicultural congregations. Pan Asian churches create a supra-identity among a group of previously distinct ethnic groups[18]. It is the result of the struggle of younger generations and their solidarity with others like them from other ethnicities. This is similar to categorizing 'Latino' to include people from many nations. In most pan Asian American churches, one of the many Asian ethnicities tend to be predominant. Pyong Gap Min observed that most pan Asian churches do not appeal to South East Asian, South Asian and Filipinos and concludes that qualifiers like East Asian and South Asian are more accurate in describing pan ethnic congregations. Many of the Chinese and Korean leaders have served the Asian Indian community well in casting a vision for generational ministry and passion for serving God.

Asian American women experience a liminal existence on account of their "double bind" or double minority status. The power structures within churches typically exclude women from leadership and religious authority. The desire for autonomy from oppressive church structures motivates many Asian Americans to split off and start their own congregations. The second generation Asian American churches intentionally alienate themselves from cultural baggage and rally around a common vision and a sense of community to lead its members.

Asian American women outmarry to escape the Asian patriarchal thinking; having been exposed to western ideas and a more egalitarian society, women feel trapped in Asian marriages. Asian American women outmarry at a higher rate (21%) than men (11%).[19] They share similar sentiments and dilemmas with many young women in Coconut generation. Jeanette Yep articulated this struggle well in the book she co-authored with other Asian Americans,

For many of us who grew up in North America, a traditional Asian marriage is quite unappealing; it seems emotionally ungratifying, rigid and even oppressive. So in a reactionary spirit, we tend to romanticize the white, middle class American model of marriage. As with bicultural individuals, we often talk about enjoying the best of the both worlds.[20]

But what many Indian parents fear when their daughters hold such a romantic notion of western egalitarian marriages is the likelihood of divorce, which is so prevalent in western society and the shame they have to bear when the rest of the community discovers that their daughter has separated or divorced.

Renowned anthropologist Margaret Mead claimed that mass media fueled generational discontinuity in Euro-America societies and is true of all immigrant families. She worried that youth would have less and less in common with their parents and other older members of the society and concluded that the twentieth century has created "cofigurative" cultures in which young people learn more about life from their peers than from their elders.[21] With the recent technological advances, we find that more information flows horizontally within generations rather than vertically across generations. Television, Internet, mobile telephony, etc. play the role of socializing agents and create a bridge for children of immigrants into mainstream youth culture. Just as these bridges help us to connect with others like us, it is also simultaneously isolating us from others unlike us. This fragmentation and generational discontinuity has contributed to the general crisis in authority. In immigrant homes this crisis is more prominent than others. The traditional author-

> **In the modern era, power was understood as a relationship to authority.**
> **In the postmodern era, power is understood as an authority of relationship.**
> **Leonard Sweet**

ity levels of family and other institutions are eroding fast with the Coconut generation and new sources of authority are being established.

To Ponder About:

1. What are your experiences with Asian American culture or church?

2. Find out about Asian American churches in your neighborhood and network with its leaders to learn generational similarities and differences first hand.

3. What do you know of Indian Church or ministries in other countries? How are they facing the generational and cultural transitions?

4. How does Asian Indian ethnic resurgence compare with that of Asian Americans? How does this affect Christian Ministry?

5. What are some lessons from Asian American ministries for Coconut generation?

Endnotes

[1] Russell Jeong, 'Asian American Subcutlure' in *Asian American Religions*, Fenggang Yang ed. (New York: New York University Press,1999).

[2] For a more detailed study of Chinese Christianity refer Fenngang Yang's excellent book *Chinese Christian in America: Conversion, Assimilation and Adhesive Identities*, (University Park, PA: Penn State University Press, 1999).

[3] Wing Ning Pang, The Chinese American Ministry, in *Yearbook of American and Canadian Churches*, ed Kenneth B. Bedell, (Nashinville, Tenn.: Abingdon Press) 10-18.

[4] Samuel Ling, *The "Chinese" Way of Doing Things*, (Phillipsburg, NJ: Presbyterian and Reformed Publishing, 1999) 53.

[5] Tony Carnes and Fenggang Yang eds., *Asian American Religions: The Making and Remaking of Borders and Boundaries,* (New York: New York University Press, 2004).

[6] Fenggang Yang, *Chinese Christians in America* (University Park, PA: Penn State University, 1999) 51.

[7] Richard Niebuhr, *The Social Sources of Denominationalism*, (New York: Kessinger Publishing, 1929) and Pozetta, George "Introduction" in *Immigrant Religious Experience*, (New York: Taylor & Fracis, 1991).

[8] Fumitaka Matsuoka, *Out of the Silence: Emerging Themes in Asian American Churches,* (Cleveland, Ohio: United Church Press, 1995) 20.

[9] Tony Carnes and Fenggang Yang eds., *Asian American Religions: The making and remaking of Borders and Boundaries,* (New York: New York University Press, 2004) 24.

[10] Ken Fong, *Pursuing the Pearl,* (Valley Forge, PA: Judson Press, 1999) 64.

[11] The 2001 *Korean Church Directory of America* lists 3402 Korean Protestant Churches.

[12] There are many good sources to explore Korean immigration and church history. Sang Oak Cho, *A Study of Korean American Churches and their Growth in the US,* PhD diss., Fuller Theological Seminary. Sang Hyan Lee and John Moore, Eds. *Korean American Ministry*, (Louisville: Division of Congregational Ministries PC (USA), 1993)." Also check out www.kamr.org

[13] Helen Lee, Silent Exodus in *Christianity Today* August 12, 1996. 51-52.

[14] Peter Cha, *Ethnic Identity Formation and Participation in Immigrant Churches: Second Generation Korean American Experiences*, PhD diss., Garrett-Evangelical Theological Seminary and Northwestern University 2002.

[15] Young Pai, A Socio-cultural Understanding of Korean American Youth in Sang Hyan Lee and John Moore eds., *Korean American Ministry,* (Louisville, KY: Presbyterian Church (USA), 1993), 268.

[16] Won Moo Hurh and Kwang Chung Kim, Religious Participation of Korean Immigrants in the US" *Journal of the Scientific Study of Religion 29(1):19-34.*

[17] Jung Ha Kim, *Bridge Makers and Cross-bearers: Korean American Women and the Church,* (Atlanta: Scholars Press, 1997).

[18] Russell Jeong, 'Asian American Subculture' in *Asian American Religions* (New York: New York University Press, 2004).

[19] Tony Carnes and Fenggang Yang, eds., *Asian American Religions: The Making and Remaking of Borders and Boundaries*, (New York: New York University Press, 2004) 326.

[20] Jeanette Yep, Peter Cha, Susan Riessen, Greg Jao and Paul Tokonaga, *Following Jesus Without Dishonoring Your Parents: Asian American Discipleship,* (Downers Grove, IL: IV Press, 1998) 91-92.

[21] Margaret Mead, *Culture and Commitment: A Study of Generation Gap,* (Garden City, NY: Doubleday-Natural History Press, 1970) 45.

9

Laying Foundations: Theology of Ministry to Coconuts

Seek not to understand so that you may believe,
but believe so that you may understand.
– St. Augustine

In this penultimate chapter, I hope to provide some theological rocks that could shape our ministries to Asian Indians in the Western world. In no way this is a full blown theological treatise, but some helpful pointers to understand deeper issues of ministering to this group of people. Neither will this chapter furnish any programs or models of ministry, but only a broad framework within which you can shape a variety of ministries to the Coconut generation.

What I have most commonly seen in youth ministries across Asian Indian American congregations can be divided into the following broad categories. A) Youth Babysitters: flock them downstairs to the basement as their parents worship upstairs without "disturbance"; B) Youth Entertainers: playing their favorite music and games; C) Program Directors: keeping youth busy with programs and activities; D) Event Organizers: pulling together event after event; E) Idea Generators: ever bursting with the next new thing; F) Tradition Keepers: preserving how things have been done for ever; G) Care Givers: offering shoulders to cry on.

Do not misunderstand me; all of these are important aspects of youth ministry in every church and campus. But when the stakes are as high as losing a generation, I want to raise the bar for ministry to this generation everywhere. We cannot do youth ministry without giving careful theological, psychological and sociological reflection to the world of adolescents. So far in this book, we have examined many disciplines – history, sociology, psychology, anthropology, etc. and now we turn to theological issues pertinent to ministry to the Coconut generation.

Why Theology?

Youthworkers have long relied heavily on social sciences to shape their approach to ministry; disciplines like psychology, education, sociology and anthropology. Surely, each of these disciplines has contributed much to our understanding of adolescence and our educational ministry to them. We now use better methodology, learning theory, developmental psychology, psychotherapeutics and the study of subcultures to shape our ministry and have relied less on theology. I am not saying we do not need insights from these fields, but to develop a theology-centered multidisciplinary approach of ministering to youth. I have used insights from all these fields throughout this book.

Identity formation was a task that the church once claimed stake in, but in the last few decades social sciences have hijacked it. Youth ministry is traditionally considered as a sub-discipline of Christian Education, where we depended on educational theories, learning styles, programs and curriculums. The Western church turned to social sciences instead of theology to understand our task with the young people, delving deeply into modern "stage theories", newer programs and entertainment rather than a transformative life experience or meaningful discipleship. They were 'herded' down to the church basement and college dorms with the lat-

> **Believing in God is not the issue (for youths); believing that God matters is the issue.**
> **Kenda Dean & Ron Foster**

est creative ideas, curriculums and service projects. There is a real danger in Indian American churches and youth ministries aping some of the deviant Western models and dependence on social sciences. It is high time to reclaim a theological basis for ministry to the emerging generations.

Just as it is important to understand this generation, it is equally, if not more important to have an understanding of human nature, sin, salvation and God; together these understandings will fashion our ministries to them. To view youth ministry as practical theology suggests an entirely new direction for the church – "anchoring youth ministry in the life, death and resurrection of Christ; relies less on the order of human development and more on order of salvation."[1]

Practical Theology[2] as a field was first developed by German philosopher Friedrich Schleiermacher (1768-1834). Simply put, practical theology is a critical reflection on the actions of the church in light of the gospel of Jesus Christ and Christian tradition. Don Browning defines it as "the reflective process which the church pursues in its effort to articulate the theological grounds of practical living in a variety of areas such as youth, work, sexuality, marriage, aging and death."[3] He developed a compelling model from what he called practical reason with an "outer envelope and an inner core"[4], in which he integrates theory and practice in an ongoing process of action and reflection. Ray Anderson revised the model to address the lack of Christological concentration at the core and a Trinitarian theology at the foundation. The Christopraxis he added to the core is "the continuing ministry of Christ through the power and presence of the Holy Spirit."[5] Why do we need such an approach to youth ministry? Most often, practical matters of leading and serving youth are detached from theological reflection, and as a result both ends have been impoverished. We need to develop a biblically and theologically informed and integrated approach to theory and practice of youth ministry in the power of the Spirit of Jesus Christ.

Displacement: Bridge, Pilgrim or Diaspora Theology

Many immigrant communities around the world have drawn much inspiration and encouragement from stories of migrants from the scriptures. The Bible seems to be filled with nomadic wanderers like Abraham, Isaac, Jacob, Joseph, David, Paul, etc. Nomads are always departing and always arriving. They have no homes, but roam from place to place. There is no starting point just as there is no goal to reach; every place of arrival is a point of departure. Other current metaphors of people on the move are vagabond, stroller, or tourist.

Abraham was actually the first Biblical immigrant who lived in many foreign countries. He was a great success at it. He built bridges with foreign communities and became the father of the three major religions of the world: Judaism, Islam, and Christianity. His strategy was "wherever he went he built an altar and built a bridge" to connect with God and different cultures. In this way, he overcame cultural differences, generational differences, and faith differences. Barnabas was another bridge builder in the New Testament. He invited Paul to be his co-worker at Barnabas' church when most early Jewish Christians rejected Paul as a persecutor of

Christ followers. He introduced Paul to Peter and other disciples. His greatest contribution in Christian missions was in building bridges to connect Paul with apostles. I tend to think that without Barnabas' effort to connect Paul with others, Paul would not have been accepted by Peter and the other disciples. As a result, Paul's activities and missions would have been limited or delayed. But by building bridges across the generational and cultural gaps between the disciples and Paul, Barnabas played a crucial role in the early spread of the gospel of Jesus Christ. Because of Barnabas, the Christian church and Jesus' mission transferred smoothly from Peter to Paul and to Timothy and Titus.

Standing in the gap to bridge the widening gulf between generations, culture and worldview are important pieces of ministry in immigrant churches. They enable all to see beyond peculiarities of people to capture the wonder of God's continual work in every era, culture, and generation.

The emerging generation of immigrant sometimes fail to appreciate the traveler, wanderer, Promised Land, or pilgrim metaphor for themselves, although it might have been true of their parents. For them it is not as much a geographical dislocation, but a cultural displacement. The Diaspora theology is more aptly suited for the emerging generation, which deals with the complexity of multiple cultural influences, bicultural identity and global network of communities.

God in his sovereignty uses dispersion of people for the progress of the gospel into foreign territories like Judea and Samaria (Acts 8:1). The Diaspora Jews created a platform for Paul's ministry to the Gentiles. The epistles of James and 1 Peter were written to address the challenges and needs of the Jewish Diaspora. The cultural uprootedness can be a positive force to greater openness to the gospel and pursuing an identity beyond ethno-cultural realities. With a global vision, the emerging generation is strategically placed to fulfill the Great Commission "to the ends of the earth" (Mt 28:20).

Incarnation: Marginal Embrace

Because of the relational nature of youth ministry, many have adopted incarnational ministry as their paradigm of working with the youth, ministry in which God enters the world through human beings just as Jesus came into the world through a Jewish teenager. The incarnational ministry entails becoming Godbearers[6] and birthing Jesus into the lives of our kids, churches and the world. The incarnational ministry elevates the relationship driven paradigm to provide a theological character to the youth ministry. But the danger of youthworkers projected as the incarnate one is real and when they fumble in their walk with God, the faith of the kids follows the downward spiral. We must make the distinction that only God can be Incarnate and as we live faithfully in order to be more Christ-like and let youth see Christ beyond us so that they follow him and are obedient to him.

A theology of marginality deals with both the central perspective of marginality (neither/nor) and the self affirming perspective of marginality (both/and).[7] Jesus possessed dual identity (divine, human), experienced the crisis of belonging to two worlds at the same time and thus offers the best model for us. Jesus was a marginalized person – born of an unwed teenage girl, born far from his hometown in a manger, visited by Eastern Magi instead of his own ethnic community, forced to seek shelter in Egypt etc. Incarnation – leaving his heavenly abode to be born as a human baby in this world, is an experience of margins. His social, class, economic, political and ethnic orientation made him a marginal person. He experienced loneliness, felt abandoned by his Father on the cross, God is not central to those who seek the center, but

God is center to those who seek marginality, because the real center is the creative core, the margin of marginality – Jesus Christ.[8] The self-giving, self-emptying model of Jesus' ministry beckons us to deny ourselves and take up the cross and follow him.

Mirosalf Volf introduced us to the concept of embrace: it is more than giving "others" their due, and even more than reconciliation. Embrace stand for reaching out to "others" and finding a place within ourselves as individuals and cultures for others while still remaining ourselves. This is a powerful paradigm for ministry amidst the liminal existence of emerging generations of immigrants in America, which takes the hybrid nature of their selves more comprehensively.

Transformation: Socialization Is Not Enough

The immigrant Indian churches in America have focused more on cultural and religious socialization than transformation intrinsic to the human spirit's search for intimacy in the context of ultimacy. Socialization may be defined as "all the processes, both conscious and unconscious, both interpersonal and socio-cultural, by which people become inducted and inculcated into the larger contexts of society.[9] One of the leading voices on transformational vocabulary and the theological perspective on human development has been Dr. James E. Loder. He argued that "under the aegis of *Spiritus Creator,* the logic of transformation itself is transformed" to become what he called "convictional knowing," which is "human knowing that approximates Christ's own knowing of the human situation, revealed to human beings Spirit-to-spirit, through the gospel by faith."[10]

The Indian immigrant churches attempt to socialize their young people even as young people rebel against such domestication.

Loder criticized the dispassionate dishonesty and lack of integrity that passes for maturity in our culture and in our congregations and denominations under the power of socialization. The church may be guilty of being consumed with "tension-reduction and pattern maintenance" priority intrinsic to the social construction of reality and thus domesticating the church's potential for prophetic witness to society.[11] There is something "abnormal" about "normal" socialization towards pattern-maintaining equilibrium and youths, more than anyone else, are deeply aware of it, even when they cannot precisely locate it. Loder called normal human development and normal ideas of maturity "subnormal" from a convictional perspective.[12] One way they fight social conformity to the church is by dropping out of spiritually domesticated congregations in droves.

For Loder, the relational transformation in *Koinoinia* means that all normal relationships (including those embodied in socialized religious practices and family role structures) must be affirmed, crucified and resurrected. He posits a new, re-centered identity for adolescents grounded in the Reality of Christ and it supports Moltmann's conviction that "Christian identity can be understood only as an identification with the Crucified Christ, to the extent to which one has accepted the proclamation that in him God has identified [God's] self with the godless and those abandoned by God, to whom one belongs. If Christian identity comes into being by this double process of theological identification, then it is clear that such identity cannot be described in terms of human faith alone, nor can it be protected against decay by correct doctrinal formulae, repeatable rituals and set patterns of moral behavior."[13]

Apostle Paul wrote to the Romans, "Do not conform any longer to patterns of this world, but be transformed by the renewing of your mind." (Rom 12:2). In other words, do not be socialized or squeezed into sinful customs of this world, but be radically altered from the inside out into a new creation in Christ.

Missions: Paradigm for Ministry and Church

For those outside of the Coconut generation and those within it, missions is a compelling paradigm for ministry to the generation. Some have argued that all youth ministry, by it's vary nature and growing discontinuity with rest of the church, is inherently akin to the task of cross-cultural mission. The vast resources on theology of mission and missiology could come in the aid of youth ministry.[14]

Missionaries are lifelong students of people, culture and what Spirit is doing in the world. We must not only study second generation, their culture and popular culture of our times, but also sensitive to what Spirit is stirring up among them. The Catholic theologian, Tom Beaudoin argues that popular culture has served as the primary medium through which a new generation of Americans made sense of their lives. As this generation become disillusioned with traditional sources of meaning and authority such as the state, the educational system, the family and the Church, the popular culture became the "surrogate clergy" that guided and formed this generation.[15] Just as intentional missiological engagement with cultures of developing world led to the emergence of new theologies that has enriched the meaning of Christian faith and practices, we must decisively engage new cultures of a new generation and develop new missiological insights resulting in enrichment of American Christianity as well as Indian Christianity.

Our churches must move from the paradigm of cultural churches to missional churches for the new generation. The

Coconut generation has also fallen prey to the thinking, "what do I get from the church?" Church has become "a vendor of religious services and goods." A consumeristic viewpoint is gaining ground with the second generation - they come to church to be fed; to have their needs met through quality programs, people, and to some extent to be entertained. Many have written off the meaningless repetition, rituals, liturgy or songs, unfamiliar languages, lack of genuine spirituality, superficiality of people and leaders. Also, church service with professional music, lighting, skits, presentation, videos, communication, and technology which makes congregation mere spectators and hinders us from a transformational encounter with the Divine Being. There is more to it than mere style, form or format, but their discontent with Sunday mornings and a deep yearning for genuine experience with God is clearly evident. A changing paradigm like culture cannot be central to defining church, though it might help socialization of immigrant communities. We must look to the paradigm of missions – the unchanging work of God in our world.

The missional church[16] is seen as a body of people sent on a mission who gather in community for worship, encouragement, and teaching from the Word that supplements what they are feeding themselves through the week. The major difference between the consumer churches to missional church is that in the former "I *go* to church" and in the later "I *am* the church". We must resist the tendency to become a cultural club or consumer-oriented place by keeping the mission in the forefront of all that we do. We must go back to the beginning of the church to rediscover its original intended purpose and redefine church to the Coconut generation. Somebody rightly said that ministry in the 21st century is going to be more like that of the 1st century than the 20th century. We have much to learn from how Paul's missional theology challenged the institutional theology of the Jerusalem church.

Power of the Gospel: Good News for Both Worlds

Christendom places high value on law, right and wrong, and morality which, in turn, shaped the Western worldview and vice versa. The Christian theology emerged out of early Church fathers who lived and worked in the Roman Empire within a Greek philosophical context, which provided a helpful way of understanding sin as essentially guilt – a judicial or forensic concept. To this understanding Christ is presented as one who offers forgiveness and pardon. Thus, justification is a key theological concept in dealing with the problem of guilt. Paul used the legal term in Rom 5:18 to explain what Christ has done for us. But in Eastern societies which are shame based, adoption is the key theological concept in dealing with the problem of shame. Shame destroys our self-identity within the family and community. Adoption restores what has been disinherited (Gal. 4).

In Genesis 3, at the event of the original sin, there are three basic emotions – shame, guilt and fear. Understanding how these emotions shaped different societies and cultures around the world is crucial for Christian ministry. Asian societies are mostly shame based, the Western world emphasizes on guilt and the Middle Eastern world fear/honor based. The Bible uses both concepts of guilt and shame as the result of human sin. The word guilt or guilty is used only 27 times, while the word shame appears 225 times in the Old and New Testaments.[17] The popular Western interpretation of the fall as guilt is made of decree, disobedience, and death. God had placed Adam and Eve in the Garden and had given them a standard to live by. God gave them everything they needed, including a warning – "But you must not eat from the tree of the knowledge of good and evil, for when you eat of it you will surely die." (Gen 2:17, NIV). They failed to keep the warning and disobeyed his commandment. The consequence of Adam and

Eve's sin was death – a spiritual separation from God.

When Adam and Eve sinned in the Garden of Eden, they first felt shame, not guilt. We read in the last verse of Gen 2, in the perfect state before the fall, "The man and woman were both naked and they felt no shame." (NIV) After the fall, we read in Gen 3:7 – "The eyes were opened and they realized they were naked; so they sewed fig leaves together and made coverings for themselves." (NIV) The word used for naked is different in each case. Adam and Eve's response is even more interesting. They covered up their nakedness. In shame based cultures, our immediate response to sin is to cover up. In a state of shame we cover up who we are. Similar to the fig leaves in the case of Adam and Eve, all our attempts to cover up falls short of the permanent solution to the shame we experience. Finally, God takes initiative to solve our problem of shame that we experience as a result of sin. In Gen 3:21, "The Lord God made garments of skin for Adam and his wife and clothed them." This was a pointer to God's grand plan of salvation through Jesus Christ to provide covering for sins of all humanity.

> **Do not be afraid;**
> **you will not suffer shame.**
> **Do not fear disgrace;**
> **you will not be humiliated.**
> **You will forget the shame of your youth**
> **and remember no more the**
> **reproach of your widowhood.**
> **Isaiah 54:4 (NIV)**

Guilt is the self-condemnation resulting from the violation of internalized convictions of right and wrong; whereas shame is the feeling of group condemnation resulting from an expected societal or divine norm. Guilt is a feeling and/or a condition occurring when one has broken or not kept a divine or human law. On the other, hand shame is a feeling and/or a condition resulting from a shortcoming in one's state of being either before peers, somebody higher in the social hierarchy, or even God. In both there is a subjective and objective, real and imagined components to them.

In Jesus Christ alone, we find the perfect and permanent solutions to the problems of guilt and shame. Jesus bore our guilt and he bore our shame. He endured the cross, scorning its shame. (Heb 2:2). Both forgiveness and adoption are available to us through Jesus Christ. What grace is to forgiveness, love is to adoption. The freedom that we experience from guilt due to Jesus' substitutionary sacrifice in guilt-based culture is analogous to the restoration of relationship and sense of belonging we experience in shame-based culture due to Jesus' mediation.

The experience of Americanized Asian Indian is a combination of both guilt and shame, making the task of presenting the gospel of Jesus Christ harder. They strangely feel the best and worst of both guilt and shame based cultures. The bicultural communities exhibit a hybridization of our understanding of human nature and sin. How I praise God that the gospel of Jesus Christ offers solutions for all expressions of sins, including both shame and guilt – every combination of it and to any degree. We must be like Paul in Galatians or John in his gospel and epistles. Our gospel presentation to the Coconut generation must include both aspects of the cultures that shape them.

Post modernity: Whatever

For some postmodernity is a new word, but others might be saying, "don't tell me all this is postmodernity!" No matter what you know or have read about this or not, we better start learning more about it. It might seem fuzzy in the beginning and outright an contradiction of concepts; but keep chewing it for a while and I can assure you that you will begin to get it. I remember a few years ago a youth speaker friend of mine warned me, "Without understanding postmodernity, we do not have a ministry with the second generation of Indians in the West."

Many church leaders make the mistake of seeing postmodernism as a narrow, generational issue and hope that people grow out of it. But it is more than a fad and the trend seems to indicate otherwise. When you explore the subject further, you come to realize that postmodernism has all the well developed philosophical, aesthetic and cultural underpinning that characterizes broad periods of time in history. I have listed a few resources in the bibliography for you to peruse. A good place to begin is Stanley Grenz's *A Primer on Postmodernism.*

The worldview and culture of modernism lay emphasis on science and technology, a belief that knowledge is good and certain; a single moral standard of truth as absolute, the value of individualism and that thinking, learning and beliefs should be determined systematically and logically. But the emerging worldview and culture is pursuing what is beyond modernity. It holds that there is no single universal worldview. Therefore truth is not absolute and many of the qualities embraced by modernism no longer hold the value or influence they once did. A good description of the postmodern world was given by Dave Tomlinson, "..a world which understands itself through biological rather than mechanistic models; a world where people see themselves as belonging to the environment rather than apart from it or over it. A world distrustful of institutions, hierarchies, centralized bureaucracies and male dominated organizations. It is a world where networks and local grassroot activities take precedence over large scale structures and grand designs; a world in which the book age is giving way to the screen age; a world hungry for spirituality yet dismissive of systematized religion. It is a world in which image and reality are so deeply intertwined that it is difficult to draw the line between the two."[18]

What does all this postmodernism mean for ministry to the Coconut generation? Here are some: This generation views spirituality from a pluralistic viewpoint; they are drawn more to experiential and even mystical experiences rather than rational ones; more open and tolerant view on sexuality; more image driven than words; interactivity in communication; use of creativity etc. All of these and other issues have profound implications on how we deal with the Coconut generation.

Emerging Ministries: New Wineskins

During his earthly ministry, Jesus often challenged the old order of faith practices of his day. God is doing a new thing and it is time to leave behind old habits and find new ways of responding to God's grace. Change of old order is inevitable and the analogy Jesus used to usher the start of the new order was wineskin. The disciples of John the Baptist approached Jesus and asked, "Why do we and the Pharisees fast, but your disciples do not fast?"

Jesus' reply was pithy: "No one sews a piece of unshrunk cloth on an old cloak, for the patch pulls away from the cloak, and a worse tear is made. Neither is new wine put into old wineskins; otherwise, the skins burst, and the wine is spilled, and the skins are destroyed; but new wine is put into fresh wineskins, and both are preserved." (Mt 9:14-17)

Fasting represented an old way of responding to God. The way fasting was done was indicative of old religiosity and is is incompatible with the joy with which people should react to what God was doing through Jesus. He was against the legalisms of his day that robbed the spiritual disciplines of their essence and power for transformation. Today is a new day. New days demand radically new ways of acting. His focus was not on law, but on relationships. This was a radical departure from the religious practices at that time.

To understand the imagery, we must travel back in time before the use of glass bottles and steel canisters for fermenting wine; People used bags made of animal skins to ferment wine. When grape juice was poured into new animal skin bags, they could stretch and expand. On the contrary, when grape juice was poured into old, dried out skin that were inflexible and already stretched to the limit, the fermenting process causes a tear and wine would be spilled out. Thus, when new wine is placed in old skin bags, both wine and bags are destroyed. But the new wineskin as well as the old have their own purposes. The process of fermentation could be compared with the adolescent life stage. Once the adolescent identities are fermented, they could safely be preserved in old wineskins. So the old wineskins do have many uses, but fermenting new wine is not one of them! Large containers of wine are usually made of old dried wineskins, which are used to store already fermented wine. The emerging generations need to be fermented in new wineskins. If we try to contain the passion of this generation in existing containers, they will create a tear and we will lose both the new content (emerging generation) and the container (institutions). We are seeing in many immigrant churches, as the new wine ferments, that it is threatening to come apart at the seams of the containers.

It would be pertinent at this juncture to do a cultural hermeneutical reading from an Indian perspective. In ancient days, wine was one of the important constituents of the sacrifice offered to the gods. Only the priestly *Brahminical* caste was allowed to make the wine in order to pay homage to gods for propitiation. As animals were worshiped in India, their skin could not be used for making wine; instead they used earthen vessels. Normally the ingredients were poured into large earthen containers and the lid was tightly tied to its mouth. Then they were kept half buried in earth for weeks and sometime for months for fermentation. Instead of vessel cracking or tearing, when the pressure builds up inside the containers due to fermentation, the lid pops off to release the pressure and sometimes the wine spills out.

If the new generation of Indian Americans are fermented properly with correct ingredients and right conditions, they could be transformed and become an offering to God. The "fermentation" of the youth is the supernatural transformation from the inside out by the Spirit of Christ. The earthen pots can be compared to the institutional immigrant churches. They are capable of transforming the new generation only when the priests (believers in Christ) place the youth into the earthen vessels and allows them to "ferment". If the lid is tied too tightly, it is sure to pop up and wine will spill out and if it is left open, it might not ferment at all! We need a new breed of priests who will take their duty of "wine-making" seriously and help our youths "ferment."

To Ponder About:

1. Do you think, theology really matters to youth ministry?

2. What are some theological issues that are critical in your ministry with the Coconut generation?

3. Have you used theological lens to gain a deeper understanding of your ministry with youth? Why or why not?

4. What are your theological reflections have you read on displacement, marginality, identity, bi-culturalism, pluralism, materialism and other "isms" in the Indian American community?

5. What are some theological rocks that shape your ministry in the immigrant churches?

Endnotes

[1] Kenda Dean, *Practicing Passion: Youth and the Quest for a Passionate Church,* (Grand Rapids: Eerdmans, 2004) 255.

[2] If you are not conversant with this field, please explore following writings for a comprehensive survey of the history and introduction to Practical Theology, see Don S. Browning, ed. *Practical Theology: The Emerging Field in Theology, Church and World* (San Francisco: Harper & Row, 1983) and Gerben Heitink, *Practical Theology: History, Theory and Action Domains* (Grand Rapids: Eerdmans, 1999)

[3] Don Browning, *The Moral Context of Pastoral care* (Philadelphia: Westminister Press, 1976) 14.

[4] Don Browning, *A Fundamental Practical Theology* (Minneapolis: Fortress, 1991) 10.

[5] Ray S Anderson, *The Shape of Practical Theology: Empowering Ministry with Theological Praxis,* (Downers Grove: IV Press, 2001) 29.

[6] To read more on this see, Kenda Dean & Ron Foster, *The Godbearing Life,* (Nashville: Upper Room Books, 1998).

[7] Jung Lee, *Marginality: The Key to Multicultural Theology,* (Minneapolis: Augsburg Fortress Publishers, 1995) 75.

[8] Ibid. 97.

[9] Peter Berger and Thomas Luckman, *The Social Construction of Reality: A Treatise in the Sociology of Knowledge* (New York: Doubleday, 1967), 130-131.

[10] James E. Loder, *The Transforming Moment,* (San Francisco: Harper & Row, 1981)

[11] Dana Wright, "Youth, Passion and Intimacy in the context of Koinonia" in *Redemptive Transformation in Practical Theology,* (Grand Rapids: Eerdmans, 2004) 155.

[12] James Loder and Jim Niehardt, *The Knight's Move: The Relational Logic of the Spirit in Theology and Science,* (Colorado Spriings: Helmers & Howard, 1992) 284.

[13] Jurgen Moltmann, *The Crucified God* (Minneapolis: Fortress Press, 1993), 19.

[14] See Peter Ward, *Youthwork and the Mission of God,* (London: SPCK, 1997).

[15] Tom Beaudoin, *Virtual Faith: The Irreverent Spiritual Quest of Generation X* (New York: Jossey-Bass, 1998) 21.

207

[16] See Darrell Guder, *The Missional Church: A Vision for the Sending of the Church in North America* (Grand Rapids: Eerdmans, 1998).

[17] James Strong, *Strong's Exhaustive Concordance of the Bible.* (New York: Abingdon Press, 1975).

[18] Dave Tomlinson, *The Post-Evangelical* (Grand Rapids: Zondervan, 2003) 75.

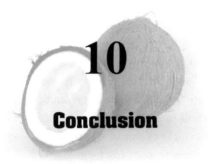

10

Conclusion

Karl Marx once said that in order to take over any nation, one must create a breach between one generation and the next, preventing the transfer of strong values, morals, and beliefs. The generational breach is more evident in children of immigrants than any other. What happens in a home and in a community soon extends to include a whole nation. The challenge of ministry to the Coconut generation will shape the future of not only our churches, but the entire Indian American community and the future of both nations.

The future of Indian American Christianity in the 21st century depends on practical, living examples of authentic vibrant faith. It might morph into an entirely new entity from what the immigrant generation planted it to be. They might imbibe popular Western Christianity or become multicultural congregations or establish its unique cultural wrapping with a new coating.

Coming Home: The Father's Heart

Jesus was a master storyteller and the parable of the Prodigal Son is one of most loved and popular stories in the Bible found in Luke 15: 11-32. Please grab a Bible and read that story again, even if it is familiar to you. It is a story of man who had two sons; the younger one asks his father for his share and goes away to a far country; after spending all his inheritance, he ends up in a pig feeding job. There in the pigpen as he ate the pig food, he thinks of how the servants in his father's household who had more than enough good food. He eventually comes to his sense and decides to go back to father; to seek his forgiveness and work as a slave for him. But father runs to the edge of the village to welcome his wayward son. Father embraces him lovingly and throws a party to mark his sons' return. When the older brother returns home and finds out that his father is celebrating his brother's homecoming, he was distressed and angry refusing to enter inside. Father meets with him outside to plead with his firstborn to join the celebration in honor of his lost and found brother.

If taken culturally and generationally, we could associate the younger brother to the emerging generation as they have drifted away into a foreign culture and the immigrant generation to the older brother who stuck with the home culture. No matter whether you identify with the home culture or the foreign culture, the crux of the story is that both could be far from the heart of the father God. The younger brother had to get away from home to realize the heart of his father, while the older brother, even though had stayed with his father and worked for him all his life, never knew his father's heart. Neither cultural preservation nor cultural dislocation is an ideal state in itself, but knowing the heart of God and being home with him is what matters. There is a prodigal son and an older brother in all of us; we wander in far away countries and squander our cultural and spiritual inheritances; only when we hit rock bottom do we realize the richness of what home offers and we come to our senses to return; not that the culture or abundance at home is the attraction, but being home with the father. I am not saying any particular culture is better than the other, but using it figuratively.

When the prodigal son returns home, father runs to meet him while he is still a long way off; the father embraces his lost son and kisses his pig smelling face. Before he completes his well-practiced plea for pardon and request for the slave position in his household, his father calls out his servant to put the best robe, ring and sandals on his son. The prodigal son confessed that he is not worthy to be his father's son anymore, yet his father restores son-ship to him. In those days, everyone other than slaves wore sandals; ring signified authority and the robe was symbolic of wealth or royalty.

The father was a loving and compassionate man; the prodigal son's knowledge of his character brought him back; the older brother was envious of the father's compassionate gesture. Not only does the father forgive a wayward child, but he also adopts the prodigal to be his son again, thus resolving the problems of both guilt and shame cultures. This parable is an ideal story to share the gospel with the Coconut generation, as it deals with both cultures' dilemmas and offers a comprehensive solution as well.

It is my hope and prayer that Coconut generation will journey to the home of their heavenly Father, whose heart is full of extravagant love and grace and be reinstated to the rightful place of being the child again, instead being a slave in a far country.

Puja[1]: **A Living Sacrifice**

After deliberating on profound theological themes, Paul exhorted Gentile believers in Rome with practical applications in Romans chapter 12 onward. He urged, "..in view of God's mercy, to offer your bodies as living sacrifices, holy and pleasing to God – this is your spiritual act of worship." (verse 1) He was elevating the worship to a whole new level; from ritual activity to a spiritual act involving every facet of one's being including heart, mind and will. In worship, Jews offered unblemished animals as sacrifice, which were killed on the altar and shed blood provided forgiveness of the sins of the worshippers. So contrary to the dead animal sacrifices, he was pleading with his readers to be a living sacrifice – living life fully devoted, consecrated and delightful to the Lord.

The term for worship in most Indian languages is *puja*, which is considered as an act of showing reverence to a god or goddess, a spirit, or another aspect of the divine through invocations. Placing offerings to the deity is an essential part of every *puja*. During *puja*, a devotee presents gifts that, according to some traditions, the particular god or goddess likes: often flowers, special foods, grains, coconuts, or oils. In most parts of India, one of the most common and popular item during *puja* is coconut; the devotees take a whole coconut to the priest, who crushes it on the altar and is placed before the deity.

I hope and pray that Coconut generation will become living coconut sacrifices at the altar of the Living God of the Universe. They will come to experience the mercy God has shown in Jesus Christ and accept his offer of salvation by his shed blood on the cross of Calvary and live up to Paul's call to the spiritual act of worship as a generation.

Before I finish, allow me to quote one of my favorite theologians,

Dietrich Bonhoeffer. In 1934 at the age of 28, he stood before the youth delegation of the Universal Christian Council for Life and Work to suggest that the "problem" of youth ministry could not be answered by youth ministry itself (i.e. by socially established programs and innovations), but only by the Word of God: "The future of the church does not depend on youth but only on Jesus Christ; the task of young people is not reorganization of the church but listening to God's Word: the church's task is not the conquest of young people, but teaching of the Gospel."[2] How pertinent that challenge is for us in the early 21st century and may we give heed to his advice.

This project turned out to be much more than what I had initially envisaged, but I thoroughly enjoyed the process of researching and writing this book. I hope it was a blessing to you and stirred your passion to serve the emerging generations of Asian Indians. Please join the online community for further critique and discussion at www.coconutgeneration.com where I hope you will have an opportunity to let your voice be heard and meet other emerging leaders of the Coconut generation.

Godspeed!

Endnotes

[1] Means Worship in many Indian languages.

[2] Dietrich Bonhoeffer, *Gesammelte Schriften,* Band III (Munich: Chr. Kaiser Verlag, 1960) 292-293. Quoted by Dana Wright in *Redemptive Transformation In Practical Theology,* (Grand Rapids: Eerdmans, 2004).

Appendix

Demographic Data

Table A1: Global Indian Diaspora[1]

(as of December 2001 with population over 100,000)

Country	PIOs	Indian Citizens	Total
Myanmar	2,500,000	402,000	2,902,000
United Kingdom	1,200,000	1,000,000	2,200,000
USA			1,678,765
Malaysia	1,600,000	65,000	1,665,000
Saudi Arabia	-	-	1,500,000
South Africa	-	-	1,000,000
UAE	50,000	900,000	950,000
Canada	700,000	151,000	851,000
Mauritius	704,640	11,116	715,756
Trinidad & Tobago	500,000	600	500,600
Guyana	395,250	100	395,100
Fiji	336,579	250	336,829
Oman	1,000	311,000	312,000
Singapore	217,000	90,000	307,000
Kuwait	1,000	294,000	295,000
Reunion Islands	220,000	55	220,055
Netherlands	200,000	17,000	217,000
Australia	160,000	30,000	190,000
Surinam	150,306	150	150,456
Qatar	1,000	130,000	131,000
Bahrain	-	130,000	130,000
Kenya	85,000	17,500	102,500
Yemen	100,000	900	100,900

[1] Data taken from Government of India – Ministry of External Affairs, report on Indian Diaspora, Dec 2001. (www.Indiaday.org/government_policy/singhvi2.asp (accessed Mar 25, 2005).

215

Table A2: Asian Indian Population by Age and Sex 2000

Age	Number			Percent			Males per 100 females
	Total	Male	Female	Total	Male	Female	
Total population	1,678,765	893,095	785,670	100.0	100.0	100.0	113.7
Under 5 years	134,533	68,955	65,578	8.0	7.7	8.3	105.1
5 to 9 years	116,524	60,001	56,523	6.9	6.7	7.2	106.2
10 to 14 years	105,290	54,234	51,056	6.3	6.1	6.5	106.2
15 to 19 years	112,203	58,249	53,954	6.7	6.5	6.9	108.0
20 to 24 years	153,666	79,200	74,466	9.2	8.9	9.5	106.4
25 to 29 years	215,587	114,758	100,829	12.8	12.8	12.8	113.8
30 to 34 years	189,332	104,408	84,924	11.3	11.7	10.8	122.9
35 to 39 years	149,307	82,080	67,227	8.9	9.2	8.6	122.1
40 to 44 years	124,506	68,365	56,141	7.4	7.7	7.1	121.8
45 to 49 years	108,339	57,689	50,650	6.5	6.5	6.4	113.9
50 to 54 years	92,685	50,117	42,568	5.5	5.6	5.4	117.7
55 to 59 years	64,522	36,458	28,064	3.8	4.1	3.6	129.9
60 to 64 years	45,437	25,837	19,600	2.7	2.9	2.5	131.8
65 to 69 years	28,499	15,177	13,322	1.7	1.7	1.7	113.9
70 to 74 years	18,086	8,652	9,434	1.1	1.0	1.2	91.7
75 to 79 years	11,159	4,981	6,178	0.7	0.6	0.8	80.6
80 to 84 years	5,590	2,450	3,140	0.3	0.3	0.4	78.0

Table A2: Asian Indian Population by Age and Sex 2000

Age	Number			Percent			Males per 100 females
	Total	Male	Female	Total	Male	Female	
85 to 89 years	2,445	1,089	1,356	0.1	0.1	0.2	80.3
90 years and over	1,055	395	660	0.1	0.0	0.1	59.8
Under 18 years	419,428	215,662	203,766	25.0	24.1	25.9	105.8
18 to 64 years	1,192,503	644,689	547,814	71.0	72.2	69.7	117.7
18 to 24 years	202,788	104,977	97,811	12.1	11.8	12.4	107.3
25 to 44 years	678,732	369,611	309,121	40.4	41.4	39.3	119.6
25 to 34 years	404,919	219,166	185,753	24.1	24.5	23.6	118.0
35 to 44 years	273,813	150,445	123,368	16.3	16.8	15.7	121.9
45 to 64 years	310,983	170,101	140,882	18.5	19.0	17.9	120.7
45 to 54 years	201,024	107,806	93,218	12.0	12.1	11.9	115.6
55 to 64 years	109,959	62,295	47,664	6.5	7.0	6.1	130.7
65 years and over	66,834	32,744	34,090	4.0	3.7	4.3	96.1
65 to 74 years	46,585	23,829	22,756	2.8	2.7	2.9	104.7
75 to 84 years	16,749	7,431	9,318	1.0	0.8	1.2	79.7
85 years and over	3,500	1,484	2,016	0.2	0.2	0.3	73.6
Median age (years)	30.0	30.5	29.5	(X)	(X)	(X)	(X)

217

Table A3: Indian American Population by Region and State

	Total	Asian Indians	% of State Pop.	% of IA Pop.	Rank
United States	281,421,906	1,899,599	0.68%	100.00%	N/A
Northeast Region	53,594,378	625,089	1.17%	32.91%	N/A
Midwest Region	64,392,776	323,802	0.50%	17.05%	N/A
South Region	100,236,820	498,197	0.50%	26.23%	N/A
West Region	63,197,932	452,511	0.72%	23.82%	N/A
Alabama	4,447,100	8,186	0.18%	0.43%	30
Alaska	626,932	981	0.16%	0.05%	48
Arizona	5,130,632	17,042	0.33%	0.90%	18
Arkansas	2,673,400	3,820	0.14%	0.20%	37
California	33,871,648	360,392	1.06%	18.97%	1
Colorado	4,301,261	13,809	0.32%	0.73%	23
Connecticut	3,405,565	26,654	0.78%	1.40%	16
Delaware	783,600	5,691	0.73%	0.30%	34
District of Columbia	572,059	3,507	0.61%	0.18%	42
Florida	15,982,378	84,527	0.53%	4.45%	6
Georgia	8,186,453	50,734	0.62%	2.67%	11
Hawaii	1,211,537	3,145	0.26%	0.17%	44
Idaho	1,293,953	1,560	0.12%	0.08%	45
Illinois	12,419,293	133,978	1.08%	7.05%	5
Indiana	6,080,485	16,683	0.27%	0.88%	19
Iowa	2,926,324	6,358	0.22%	0.33%	33
Kansas	2,688,418	9,230	0.34%	0.49%	29
Kentucky	4,041,769	7,876	0.19%	0.41%	31
Louisiana	4,468,976	9,835	0.22%	0.52%	27
Maine	1,274,923	1,303	0.10%	0.07%	46
Maryland	5,296,486	55,245	1.04%	2.91%	9
Massachusetts	6,349,097	48,588	0.77%	2.56%	12
Michigan	9,938,444	60,236	0.61%	3.17%	8

Table A3: Indian American Population by Region and State

	Total	Asian Indians	% of State Pop.	% of IA Pop.	Rank
Minnesota	4,919,479	19,963	0.41%	1.05%	17
Mississippi	2,844,658	4,609	0.16%	0.24%	35
Missouri	5,595,211	14,028	0.25%	0.74%	22
Montana	902,195	531	0.06%	0.03%	51
Nebraska	1,711,263	3,753	0.22%	0.20%	40
Nevada	1,998,257	6,756	0.34%	0.36%	32
New Hampshire	1,235,786	4,258	0.34%	0.22%	36
New Jersey	8,414,350	180,957	2.15%	9.53%	3
New Mexico	1,819,046	3,802	0.21%	0.20%	38
New York	18,976,457	296,056	1.56%	15.59%	2
North Carolina	8,049,313	29,283	0.36%	1.54%	14
North Dakota	642,200	927	0.14%	0.05%	49
Ohio	11,353,140	43,119	0.38%	2.27%	13
Oklahoma	3,450,654	9,940	0.29%	0.52%	26
Oregon	3,421,399	11,650	0.34%	0.61%	25
Pennsylvania	12,281,054	62,616	0.51%	3.30%	7
Rhode Island	1,048,319	3,593	0.34%	0.19%	41
South Carolina	4,012,012	9,578	0.24%	0.50%	28
South Dakota	754,844	727	0.01%	0.04%	50
Tennessee	5,689,283	14,548	0.26%	0.77%	21
Texas	20,851,820	142,689	0.68%	7.51%	4
Utah	2,233,169	3,800	0.17%	0.20%	39
Vermont	608,827	1,064	0.17%	0.06%	47
Virginia	7,078,515	54,781	0.77%	2.88%	10
Washington	5,894,121	28,614	0.49%	1.51%	15
West Virginia	1,808,344	3,348	0.19%	0.18%	43
Wisconsin	5,363,675	14,800	0.28%	0.78%	20
Wyoming	493,782	429	0.09%	0.02%	52
Puerto Rico	3,808,610	12,369	0.32%	0.65%	24

Bibliography

General:

Alexander, George P. *New Americans: The Progress of Asian Indians in America*, Los Angeles, CA: P&P Enterprises, 1997.

Alexander, Meena *The Shock of Arrival*, Boston: South End Press, 1996.

Augenbraum, Harold & Stavans, Ilan eds. *Growing up Latino: Memoirs & Stories,* New York: Houghton Mifflin Co., 1993.

Bandon, Alexandra *Asian Indian Americans,* Parsippany, NJ: New Discovery Books, 1995.

Bacon, Jean *Life Lines: Community, Family and Assimilation Among Asian Indian Immigrants,* New York: Oxford University Press, 1996.

Carnes, Tony and Yang, Fenggang eds. *Asian American Religions: The Making and Remaking of Borders and Boundaries,* New York: New York University Press, 2004.

Chan, Scheng *Asian Americans: An Interpretive History,* Boston: Twayne Publishers, 1991.

Chandrasekar, S. ed. *From India to America,* La Jolla, CA: Population Institute, 1982.

Dasgupta, Sathi Sengupta *On the Trail of an Uncertain Dream: Indian Immigrant Experience in America*, New York: AMS Press, 1989.

Fenton, John Y. *Transplanted Religious Traditions: Asian Indians in America*, New York: Praeger Publishers, 1988.

Fong, Timothy P. *The Contemporary Asian American Experience: Beyond the Model Minority*, Englewood Cliff, NJ: Prentice Hall, 2002.

Gordon, Susan *Asian Indians*, New York: Franklin Watts, 1990.

Holli, Melvin G. & Jones, Peter D'A. *Ethnic Chicago: A Multicultural Portrait – 4th edition*, Grand Rapids, MI: Wm. B. Eerdmans Publishing, 1995.

Jensen, Joan, *The Passage from India: Asian Indian Immigration in North America*, New Haven, CT: Yale University Press, 1988.

Kumar, Amitava *Passport Photos,* Los Angeles: University of California Press, 2000.

Leonard, Karen Isaksen *The South Asian Americans,* Westport, CT: Greenwood Press. 1997.

Maira, Sunaina Marr *Desis in the House: Indian American Youth Culture in New York City,* Philadelphia: Temple University Press, 2002.

Pradhan, Sachin N. *India in the United States: Contributions of Indian and Indians in the United States of America*, Bethesda, MD: SP Press Intl, 1996.

Prasad, Leela ed. *Live Like the Banyan Tree*: *Images of the Indian American Experience*, Philadelphia: Balch Institute for Ethnic Studies, 1999.

Prashad,Vijay *The Karma of Brown Folk,* University of Minnesota Press., 2000.

Rangaswamy, Padma *Namaste America: Indian Immigrants in an American Metropolis*, University Park: Penn State University Press, 2000.

Saran, Parmatma *The Asian Indian Experience in the United States*, Cambridge, MA: Schenkman, 1985.

Min, Pyong Gap *Asian Americans: Contemporary Trends and Issues,* Los Angeles, CA: Sage, 1995.

Scupin, Raymond ed. *Race and Ethnicity: Anthropological Focus on United States and the World*, Englewood Cliff, NJ: Prentice Hall, 2003.

Takaki, Ronald *Strangers from a Different Shore: A History of Asian Americans,* New York: Penguin Books, 1989.

Takaki, Ronald *Indian in the West: South Asians in America,* New York: Chelsea House Publishers, 1995.

Wei, William *The Asian American Movement*, Philadelphia: Temple University Press, 1993.

Ministry & Church:

Bellah, Robert *Habits of the Heart: Individualism and Commitment in American Life*, Berkley: University of California Press, 1985.

Beyer, Peter *Religion and Globalization*, London: Sage, 1995.

Cha, Peter Kang, Steve and Lee, Helen eds. *Growing Healthy Asian American Churches*, Downers Grove, IL: IV Press, 2006.

Fong, Ken U. *Pursuing the Pearl: Resource for Multi-Asian Ministry*, Valley Forge, PA: Judson Press, 1999.

Ng, David ed. *People on the Way: Asian North Americans Discovering Christ, Culture and Community*, Valley Forge, PA: Judson Press, 1996.

Lee, Jung Young *Marginality: The Key to Multicultural Theology*, Minneapolis: Fortress Press, 1995.

Lee, Sang Hyan and Moore, John eds. *Korean American Ministry*, Division of Congregational Ministries PC (USA), 1993.

Ling, Samuel *The 'Chinese' Way of Doing Things: Perspective on American Born Chinese and the Chinese church in North America,* China Horizon, 1999.

Min, Pyong Gap *Changes and Conflicts: Korean Immigrant Families in New York*, Boston: Allyn and Bacon, 1998.

Min, Pyong Gap *Religions in Asian America: Building Faith Communities,* California: Alta Mira Press, 2002.

Volf, Miroslav *Exclusion & Embrace: A Theological Exploration of Identity, Otherness and Reconciliation,* Nashville, Abingdon Press, 1996.

Williams, Raymond Brady *Religions of Immigrants from India and Pakistan: New threads in the American Tapestry*, New York: Cambridge University press, 1988.

Williams, Raymond Brady *Christian Pluralism in the United States,* Cambridge: Cambridge University Press, 1996.

Wilson, Sandra *Released from Shame: Moving Beyond the Pain of the Past*, Chicago: IV Press, 2002.

Wuthnow, Robert *The Restructuring of American Religion,* Princeton, NJ: Princeton University Press, 1988.

Yang, Fenggang *Chinese Christians in America: Conversion, Assimilation and Adhesive Identities*, University Park, PA: Penn State University Press, 1999.

Emerging Generation:

Crespo, Orlando *Being Latino in Christ: Finding Wholeness in Your Ethnic Identity,* Downers Grove: IL: IV Press, 2003.

Dean, Kenda and Foster, Ron *The Godbearing Life: The Art of Soul Tending in Youth Ministry,* Nashville: Upper Room Books, 1998.

Dunn, Richard R. & Senter III, Mark eds. *Reaching a Generation for Christ,* Chicago, IL: Moody Press, 1997.

Fong, Ken *Insights for Growing Asian American Ministries,* Los Angeles, CA: Evergrowing Publications, 1990.

Graham, Philip *The End of Adolescence,* New York: Oxford University Press, 2004.

Hong, Maria ed. *Growing up Asian American,* New York: Avon Books, 1993.

Hutchcraft, Ron *The Battle for a Generation,* Chicago, IL: Moody Press, 1996.

Lee, Lee C. and Zane, Nolan W.S. eds. *Handbook of Asian American Psychology,* Thousand Oaks, CA: Sage Publications, 1998.

Lin, Tom *Losing Face and Finding Grace: 12 Bible Studies for Asian Americans,* Downers Grove, IL: IV Press, 1996.

Min, Pyong Gap *The Second Generation: Ethnic Identity Among Asian Americans,* California: Alta Mira Press, 2002.

Nam, Vickie *YELL-Oh Girls! Emerging Voices Explore Culture, Identity and Growing Up Asian American,* New Tork: Harper Collins Books, 2001.

Ng, Donald ed. *Asian Pacific American Youth Ministry,* Valley Forge, PA: Judson Press, 1988.

Tokunaga, Paul *Invitation to Lead: Guidance for Emerging Asian American Leaders,* Downers Grove: IL: IV Press, 2003.

Uba, Laura *Asian Americans: Personality Patterns, Identity and Mental Health,* New York: The Guilford Press, 1994.

Wong, Kevin Scott and Chan, Scheng eds. *Claiming America: Constructing Chinese American Identities During the Exclusion Era,* Philadelphia: Temple University Press, 1998.

Yep, Jeanette and Cha, Peter eds. *Following Jesus Without Dishonoring Your Parents,* Downers Grove, IL: IV Press, 1998.

URL of Indian American Churches/Ministries:

1. Assemblies of God - www.cicag.org
2. Boston Bengali Church - www.safne.com/biswas.htm
3. Calvary Bible Church – www.calvarybiblechurchdallas.com
4. Campus Crusade for Christ – www.ccci.org
5. Church of South India – www.csichurch.com
6. Ethnic America Network - www.ethnic-america.net
7. Gospel of Asia – www.gfa.org
8. Gujarati Christian Fellowship – www.gcfponline.org
9. India Gospel Outreach – www.indiago.org
10. Indian Catholic Church – www.IndiaCatholic.com
11. Indian Orthodox Church – www.stgregorios.com
12. Indian Christian Portal – www.IndiaChristian.com
13. Indian Christianity Portal – www.IndianChristianity.org
14. International Student International – www.isi.org/
15. Intervarsity Christian Fellowship – www.ivcf.org
16. Kananaya Catholic Youths - www.kcylna.org
17. Mar Thoma Church – www.marthomachurch.com
18. Navigators – www.navigator.org/
19. North America Church of God – www.nacog.net
20. Nondenominational Church of India – www.churchofindia.com
21. Orthodox Youth Movement – www.mgocsmamerica.org
22. Overseas Friends of Evangelical Union – www.ofeusi.org
23. Pentecostal Church in North America Keralites – www.pcnak.org
24. Pentecostal Youth Fellowship of America – www.pyfa.org
25. Punjabi Christian fellowship – www.punjabimasihichurch.org
26. Ramesh Richard Evangelism & Church health – www.rreach.org
27. Ravi Zacharias International Ministries – www.rzim.org
28. Reaching Indians Ministires Intl. – www.rimi.org
29. South Asian Fellowship – www.safne.com
30. South Asian Friendship Center – www.safcbookstore.com
31. South Asian Global Convention – www.SouthAsianConnection.com
32. Syro Malabar Church - members.aol.com/smalabar
33. Tamil Church – www.tamilchurch.org
34. Telugu Church – www.tcfnj.com
35. United Evangelical Christian Fellowship – www.uecf.net
36. Urbana Student Mission Conference - www.Urbana.org

Websites:

1. US Census data - factfinder.census.gov
2. Demography - www.Indiademographics.com
www.AmericanDemographics.com
3. Immigration and Naturalization Services – www.ins.gov
4. Indian Embassy – www.IndianEmbassy.org
5. Global Migration Studies - www.MigrationInformation.org
6. Global Organization of People of Indian Origin – www.gopio.org
7. *Pravasi Bharati Divas* (Overseas India Day) – www.indiaday.org
8. Congressional Caucus on India and Indian Americans in United States –
www.usindiafriendship.net/congress/caucus

Newspapers & Periodicals:

1. East West Times – www.eastwesttimes.com
2. India Abroad – www.IndiaAbroad.com
3. India Bulletin – www.indiabulletinusa.com
4. India Currents – www.IndiaCurrents.com
5. India Living - www.indialiving.net
6. India New England News - www.indianewengland.com
7. India Post - www.indiapost.com
8. India Reporter – www.IndiaReporter.com
9. India Tribune – www.IndiaTribune.com
10. India West – www.IndiaWest.com
11. Indian Express – www.iexpressusa.com
12. Little India - www.littleindia.com
13. News India Times - www.newsindia-times.com